How to cope with neighbour stress

Janet Haines
Mandy Matthewson

Acknowledgements:
Steven Haines
Robyn Cartledge
Coverart designed by Freepik
(www.freepik.com)

This workbook offers suggestions on how to cope with the stress of dealing with neighbours. We do not guarantee that these suggested strategies will resolve all psychological symptoms. You may wish to seek alternative assistance from a mental health professional.

How to cope with neighbour stress
Janet Haines & Mandy Matthewson
Copyright © 2025
ISBN: 978-1-923573-14-7

About the authors

Dr Janet Haines has a PhD in Clinical Psychology and has worked as an academic and researcher for 17 years, and in private practice for 30 years helping people facing life problems.

Dr Mandy Matthewson is a Clinical Psychologist, educator and researcher with more than two decades of experience supporting people through life's toughest challenges.

For R who found that peace came not from moving house,
but from simply stepping away from the chaos.

Table of contents

Table of contents 5
Introduction 9
Types of problems 10
    Nosy neighbours and stalkers 10
    Rule breakers 11
    Noisy neighbours 12
    Complaining neighbours 12
    Messy neighbours 13
    Fence line intrusion 14
    Threatening neighbours 15
    The company they keep 15
Power imbalances 17
    Authoritarian neighbours 17
    Dangerous neighbours 17
    Longer-term residents 18
    Intimidators and bullies 19
Provocations and escalations 20
    Demands 20
    Ignoring reasonable expectations 20
    Refusing to compromise 21
    A change in attitude 21
    An escalation of conflict 22
    Your contribution to the escalation 22
Maintaining civility and understanding your rights 24
    Goal of keeping the peace 24
    Standing up for your rights 24
    Understanding your rights 25
The trap of anticipating wrongdoing 30
    Avoiding expectations of wrongdoing 30
    Incorrect interpretations 31
    Aggravation of your emotional state 31
Understanding individual differences 33
    Your values versus the values of others 33

Whose value system is right?	34
Traditional versus unconventional	35
Adopting a non-judgmental stance	36
What should I tolerate?	37
Deliberate versus accidental provocations	37
Learn what the law says	38
Local government regulations	38
Who to call for assistance	38
Negotiated outcomes	38
Taking advantage of available avenues	38
Notion of justice and injustice	40
It is only fair…	40
Feeling of injustice	41
Assumptions underlying this feeling of injustice	41
Who is in control?	43
Believing others should change to meet our needs	43
Personal change feels like defeat	43
Personal change is your strength	44
Who will be the winner?	45
Choosing a win-lose approach	45
Us-versus-them attitude	45
Choosing a win-win approach	46
Managing your environment	48
Protecting your space	48
Physical barriers	48
Psychological barriers	49
Maintaining boundaries	50
Friendly or neutral approach	50
Limit interactions	51
Focus on your own space	52
Extinguishing behaviour: The world of learning theory	53
Understanding learning theory	53
Reinforcement and rewards	54
How to respond	54
Expecting escalation	56
Perseverance is the key	57
Regulating your emotions	58

    Primary and secondary emotions 58

    Recognising and dealing with your emotions 61

    Does the size of your emotion fit your problem? 64

    The link between emotions and behaviour 71

Managing your stress and anxiety 74

    What is my nervous system doing? 74

    Range of arousal 76

    How to combat anxiety 78

    More exercises to help 85

    Managing anxiety-related thoughts 87

Managing your anger 92

    Exit and wait strategy 92

    Controlling thoughts that trigger anger 93

Managing your sleep disturbance 97

    Externally generated sleep disturbance 97

    Internally generated sleep disturbance 98

Learning to cope 103

    Coping 103

    Problem-focused coping vs. emotion-focused coping 103

    Problem-approach vs. problem-avoidance coping 104

    Identifying your preferred coping style 107

Using effective coping strategies 111

    Building your coping repertoire 111

Learning to think clearly 121

    How are our thoughts affected? 121

    Core beliefs 122

    Cognitive errors 122

    Why do we think in unhelpful ways? 139

    Underlying assumptions of logical errors 141

    Understanding automatic thoughts 144

    Catching automatic thoughts 144

    Understanding and noticing logical errors 146

    Reframing your thoughts (cognitive restructuring) 148

    Making the restructured thinking habitual 153

    Targeting the assumptions 153

Learning assertiveness skills 157

    Asking for change 157

- Learning negotiation skills 161
  - Negotiating for what you want 161
  - Readiness to compromise 162
- Keep the peace and other orders 165
  - Legal avenues 165
  - When to pursue legal avenues 165
  - Dispute resolution 165
- Letting go of past hurts 167
  - Change your self-talk 167
  - Create psychological distance 167
  - Focus on yourself 167
  - Be present focused 167
  - Be kind to yourself 168
  - Express your emotions 168
  - Accept that others may not accept responsibility 168
  - Learn self-care 168
  - Seek out supportive people 168
  - Learn to talk to others 169
  - Consider forgiveness 169
  - Seek professional assistance if needed 169
- Some final points 170
- Additional reading 171

Introduction

Your home should be your sanctuary where you feel most secure. However, the behaviour of neighbours can compromise your sense of security and your peace of mind. When you live near difficult neighbours, your quality of life is affected.

This workbook focuses on the management of your psychological reactions to the poor behaviour of a neighbour. It examines ways you can exert some influence on the situation by using psychological tactics, and it teaches you ways to manage the impact of the behaviour of a difficult neighbour on your psychological well-being. It is not a workbook about the legal action you can take to manage your difficult neighbourhood problems, although legal avenues are mentioned.

Although we explore mistakes that you might make in handling disputes with neighbours, we do not take the view that you are to blame for the problem. We do understand that, in any dispute, both parties contribute to some degree and this will be discussed. We do encourage you to take control of a situation and sometimes this is achieved by changing the way you do things rather than waiting for someone else to change their behaviour.

In examining ways that might assist you in managing what you are experiencing, let's start by looking at the variety of problems with neighbours that can develop.

Types of problems

The types of problems experienced by neighbours are extensive. They involve specific behaviours that may vary from case to case. On a continuum of severity, neighbours' behaviours may range from complaining about normal activities undertaken by you to extreme and threatening behaviour. Let's consider some of the ways in which problems with neighbours manifest.

Nosy neighbours and stalkers

Some neighbours find it difficult to control the urge to keep track of what you are doing. For some, they can feel that the neighbour is looking through their windows to see what they are doing inside their home. For others, they have a neighbour who observes them every time they leave their home. Rather than casual observation, we are referring to the type of behaviour that significantly intrudes on your privacy. The behaviour is often persistent and continues even if you try to make it clear that you are aware of their behaviour.

Nosy neighbours may also intrude more directly. They knock on your door, invite themselves into your home, and question you about where you are going, where you have been and what you are doing. Although these behaviours can seem friendly on the surface, the extent to which they intrude on your life is what makes them problematic.

> *Lucy told her friend she was being driven crazy by one of her neighbours. Lucy lived in a unit complex that allowed her to have some private garden space but with shared space as well. Because of the position of her unit, people would walk past her home on the way to their own units. In addition, visitors would come and go past her unit. That, in itself, didn't bother Lucy. What did bother her was the fact that one neighbour, who lived down the end of the property, was 'too interested' in what Lucy was doing. She told her friend that whenever she walked to the mailbox or left her home for any reason, this person would appear and observe her. Lucy said she didn't feel comfortable sitting in her unit because this person would walk back and forth, making a point of staring at Lucy through her window. Matters came to a point of tension when Lucy returned home one day from a walk to find this person standing in her flowerbed in front of her window with her face up against the glass, with her hand cupped around her face, looking into her home. Lucy demanded to know what the neighbour was doing, but the person just walked away and returned to their own home. Lucy told her friend that she believed that things had escalated since that time. This person was always hanging around, making Lucy feel uncomfortable.*

> *Lucy thought she saw the person bending down and looking through the slot in her mailbox to see if she had any mail. She caught them lifting the lid on her garbage bin she had put out on garbage collection day, poking around among the bags of garbage. When Lucy confronted her neighbour, the neighbour simply denied doing what Lucy had observed them doing.*

Rule breakers

Neighbours who break the rules tend to annoy their neighbours. They park their cars on the footpath, leave their overflowing garbage cans on the footpath and then do not bring them back after garbage collection. They park their cars in other's people car parking spaces.

For some people, the fact that other people break the rules can be disturbing. The behaviours they engage in cause inconvenience for others. Probably more importantly for some, the fact that these neighbours believe that rules should apply to everyone else but not them can aggravate the people who follow the rules.

> *Kevin and Rachael were quiet people who liked to keep to themselves. They were friendly enough with the neighbours on one side of their house, giving casual greetings whenever they happened to see each other. Kevin and Rachael considered those neighbours to be respectful of their privacy. They never caused any problems. The same could not be said for the people on the other side. These neighbours just seemed to spill out in all directions. There were multiple cars in their driveway and parked on the street. There was junk around their home. Their children would leave their bikes on the footpath. Their mailbox overflowed. However, the thing that Kevin and Rachael could not tolerate was their habit of parking on the street in a manner that blocked Kevin and Rachael's driveway. Repeatedly, Kevin and Rachael would either be unable to drive off their property when they were leaving or drive into their driveway when they were returning. At first, Kevin and Rachel asked them not to park there, pointing out the inconvenience for both Kevin and Rachael and for them when they were asked to move their car. The neighbours agreed to be more careful. However, they continued to block the access to Kevin and Rachael's home. So, Kevin pointed out to the neighbours that there were regulations saying they couldn't do what they were doing. But the neighbours continued to park that way whenever they chose. As things escalated and became more hostile, Kevin and Rachael threatened to have their car towed away and, later, threatened legal action. In response, the neighbours chose to deliberately park their car across all of the driveway, entirely blocking it and refused to move their vehicle.*

Noisy neighbours

It is difficult to live near noisy neighbours. This type of neighbour will play loud music day and night. They will argue loudly with each other so that issues that should be private are made public. They party late into the night. They start mowing their lawns early in the morning. They rev their car engines as they leave their property. Their dogs incessantly bark.

The problem is not necessarily with the nature of the behaviour but with the volume generated by the activities and/or the timing when the noise occurs. Neighbours who generate excessive noise are often considered by others to be selfish people who only consider their own needs. They do not consider the impact of their actions on those around them.

> *Ben lived in a quiet neighbourhood until his new neighbours moved in. As soon as they moved in, they started playing music loudly throughout the day and into the night. They often threw parties, with lots of people spilling out into the neighbour's yard with loud voices and music playing until the early hours of the morning. One of the neighbour's children played the drums... from early in the morning. They had two dogs that barked incessantly. Their cars were noisy, with damaged mufflers, and the children had small motorbikes that they rode around their yard that was unsuitable for such an activity. Lots of neighbours complained, but their complaints were met with hostility and threatening behaviour. The neighbours just didn't care that others were being affected by their actions.*

Complaining neighbours

Some neighbours complain excessively no matter what you have or have not done. The smallest provocation will give rise to a torrent of complaints. They complain about what you plant in your garden. They complain if you sunbake in your own backyard. They are unhappy when your children play outside. They disapprove of how often you mow your lawn. They do not like your clothes hanging on your clothesline. They are critical of how often you check your mail. Nothing escapes their attention.

You could probably disregard each of the complaints or, at least, evaluate their merits and decide if there is something that you need to do to rectify the situation. However, the large number of complaints and the breadth of their focus just encourage you to ignore them all… until you cannot do that any longer. This is because the constant criticism starts to wear you down.

> *Beth and Greg thought they lived a normal existence. They had two children who were generally well-behaved. Greg worked full-time, and Beth had a part-time job. They liked to work in their garden and were proud of the way their house looked from the street. Their friends complimented them on all the landscaping work they had done around their house. Beth and Greg knew that one of their neighbours wasn't particularly friendly. However, problems started when they received a note in their letterbox from the neighbour complaining about the noise their sheets made flapping in the wind when they hung them on the clothesline to dry. Beth and Greg didn't know what to make of the complaint but decided they would avoid hanging out their sheets to dry on very windy days. But it didn't stop there. The next complaint was that their new mailbox was inconsistent with others in the street and should be removed as a result. Then, the neighbour complained that the scent of the jasmine they had planted was drifting into the neighbour's yard and disturbing her. From a trickle, the complaints then developed into a torrent. The noise of the garage door opening was disturbing their neighbour. The children were laughing too loud when they played outside. They were told their children shouldn't play with balls just in case they bounced over the fence. They were told it was unreasonable to return home after 8 pm and drive into their driveway. They were told that their porch light was 'too shiny'. When Beth and Greg tried to reason with their neighbour, they received a complaint about them 'complaining'. Each of these complaints was laughable. However, the sheer volume of complaints caused Beth and Greg stress and unhappiness.*

Messy neighbours

There are tidy people in the world and untidy people. Neighbours who do not value tidiness can create problems for neighbours who do. While there can be problems caused by the extent of untidiness inside other people's homes (e.g, smells), it is likely to be the untidiness that spills out into areas outside their homes that cause rifts with neighbours. There can be overflowing garbage cans and bags of rubbish, old cars, stacks of things they have collected.

Many people view their surrounding neighbourhood as reflecting them as individuals. The state of their neighbourhood can influence how they perceived their status. An untidy house embedded in an otherwise tidy neighbourhood can cause an individual who keeps a tidy home to believe that the untidy house will impact on how they are viewed themselves.

Also, neighbours may have concerns that a very untidy property can impact their own property values or, at least, the saleability of their own property. They are probably justified in reasoning that their own property would be less attractive to potential buyers if the property next door was in a poor state.

> *If you drove along the street where Douglas lived, you would notice that all of the houses were neatly kept and presentable... except for one. This property did not just appear slightly less tidy than the others in the neighbourhood. It was startling how much rubbish was piled up around the house. There were piles of old tyres and old wooden planks stacked up against the house. There was a pile of used fencing wire. There was a pile of old gardening supplies – flowerpots, empty mulch bags, broken rakes, a broken wheelbarrow. There were a couple of broken chairs and an old washing machine. There were piles of rubbish that no one could identify. Complaints had been made, and the local council issued orders that the mess be cleaned up. But nothing had happened. Now, Douglas was horrified to realise there were rats nesting in the rubbish.*

Fence line intrusion

Fences provide a clear divide between one person's property and another person's property. They offer a point of demarcation between your space and another person's space. However, some neighbours are not respectful of this distinction. They allow their trees and bushes to overhang neighbours' fences. They disregard the fact that the leaves or fruit from these trees drop into your yard or on your driveway. They refuse to do anything about roots from trees in their garden cracking the concrete or blocking your drains.

In most jurisdictions, you do not need your neighbour's permission to cut back plants that are overhanging the fence on your property. However, some people are reluctant to do this because of the upset it can cause. Some people would be wary about aggravating an already difficult neighbour.

> *Lizzie's neighbour had a mulberry tree growing next to her fence. Lizzie recognised that the tree looked beautiful, but it was causing a huge problem. The tree overhung Lizzie's driveway, which was the place where Lizzie had to park her car. Its branches hung low over the fence, and they scratched the side and roof of Lizzie's car when it was windy. Lizzie carefully removed the branches that were scratching her car. However, the problem persisted. When the tree was fruiting, it dropped fruit that stained the concrete on Lizzie's driveway and the fence. As the tree grew, the problems got worse. Lizzie approached her neighbour about the problem, but the neighbour was unsympathetic and made it clear that no permission would be given to cut back the tree on Lizzie's side. Lizzie explained that the law was probably on her side and that the tree would have to be cut back. She even offered to pay for someone to come and do the work in a way that would save the tree. However, her neighbour made it clear that she would fight Lizzie in the courts if she tried to cut back the tree.*

Threatening neighbours

Some problematic neighbours are not just irritating, they are dangerous… or can certainly seem that way. They hurl verbal abuse at you whenever you leave your home. They threaten to harm you. They deliberately damage your property. They leave threatening notes.

Most people consider their home to be their sanctuary. It is particularly problematic if the behaviour of a neighbour causes you to feel unsafe in your own home or on your own property. People can feel that they are living under a constant threat.

Although these behaviours are typically illegal, people can be reluctant to report them to the police. There can be a fear of escalating conflict and acts of retribution. The expectation can be that any attempt to seek assistance can make the situation worse.

> *Warren was an elderly man who lived alone since the death of his wife. He had got along well with his previous neighbours, but after they moved to another state, problems developed. Interactions with the new neighbours were hostile from the outset. When Warren knocked on their door to introduce himself as their neighbour, he was told to get off their property. Warren withdrew and tried to stay out of their way. However, one of Warren's grandchildren kicked a ball that bounced over a low fence and came to rest on the neighbour's driveway. When the child went to retrieve his ball, he was confronted by the hostile neighbour who threatened to let his dog bite the child if he ever came onto the property again. Warren tried to explain that the child was just collecting a ball from the driveway, but he was met with aggressive threats. He was told that if he came anywhere near the property again, he would get his 'head beaten in'. If that wasn't bad enough, from that point on, things deteriorated. Every time Warren stepped outside his house, verbal abuse was hurled at him. And it was not only from the person he had initially met. The man's wife and their teenage son did the same thing. The language they used and the threats they made were very confronting for Warren. He wanted a peaceful life. He was happy to just stay out of his neighbour's way. He was even happy to apologise for whatever had upset his neighbours. He just didn't know what he had done.*

The company they keep

Sometimes, it is not only your neighbours who demonstrate problematic behaviour. It can also be the people who stay at their house or visit them. These people can be annoying and will do things like make too much noise or block your driveway entrance. They may be threatening or engaging in criminal behaviour.

It is not an easy thing to hold one person responsible for another person's behaviour. However, the fact that the problem emanates from activities on the neighbour's property would make many inclined to hold the neighbour responsible for the behaviour of their guests.

> *The people who lived next door to Cheryl and Tom were not their 'sort of people'. Nevertheless, their neighbours did not really intrude. In fact, they had hardly any direct interaction with Cheryl and Tom at all. However, they did have a problem with the people who visited their neighbours. There was a constant stream of cars and people coming and going. These people were often noisy, disrespectful, and used bad language, even when there were children around. They would arrive in the middle of the night, shining the headlights of their cars into Cheryl and Tom's home, rev their engines and use their horns as they were departing. Tom and Cheryl wouldn't have minded too much if this had been an infrequent event. But it was not. Most days and most nights, there were people coming and going. The sheer number of people and their pattern of attendance at the home of their neighbours made Cheryl and Tom wonder what they were doing there. They never stayed long. They just turned up, made a lot of noise, and then left again.*

Although there are a variety of ways neighbours' behaviour can be difficult for you to deal with, there is one feature that is consistent across all cases. That is, you are dealing with the fact that the behaviour of a neighbour is aggravating and irritating you.

Power imbalances

One of the features of neighbourhood disputes that needs to be considered is the power balance between one neighbour and another. In some cases, it is a fact that each party is well able to stand up for themselves. In other cases, there is a clear power imbalance between one person and the neighbour who is the target of their behaviour.

A power balance exists when one person makes decisions or engages in actions that advantage them and disadvantage the other person who is the target of their behaviour. Let's consider some of these power imbalances.

Authoritarian neighbours

Authoritarian neighbours are those who expect obedience to their authority and/or will try to enforce this obedience, irrespective of any personal freedoms you may be entitled to in your community or in society in general. The trouble is that, in most cases, their authority is self-appointed. They expect you to adhere to demands they have about what you do on your property. They will refer to 'neighbourhood rules' that you never agreed to and had no part in making. They set expectations that are impossible for people to achieve if they want to live their lives in a normal way.

> *The people who lived near Barry were all affected by his behaviour. On the one hand, his neighbours would laugh about him appointing himself 'king' of the neighbourhood. On the other hand, his attitude was making his neighbours stressed. That is because Barry decided he was the person who determined how everyone else should behave. He would tell people how to park their cars and how long they could park outside their own homes despite there being no regulation preventing them from doing so. He sent notes to people he believed had failed to mow their lawns often enough. When one family repainted their home, he objected to the colour they had chosen, and he sent them a letter of demand for them to change it. Nothing escaped Barry's notice... fences, garden plants, the colour of people's doors. Barry seemed to have rules about everything, and he expected others to follow them even though they played no part in formulating them. All of the rules were consistent with what he wanted and made things difficult for others.*

Dangerous neighbours

A power imbalance occurs when you have a neighbour who is dangerous or threatening. The goal of their behaviour is to intimate and keep the target of their behaviour in an inferior or subservient position to their own. The targeted person often feels they do not have the power to stand up for themselves when faced with the effort of the more aggressive neighbour to dominate.

> *Wayne's neighbour seemed to enjoy intimidating people. He was a large and imposing presence. On any occasion when they were in each other's presence, his neighbour would stand over Wayne. On the one occasion when he shook Wayne's hand, he nearly broke his the bones in his fingers. He sometimes deliberately pushed past Wayne so that Wayne stumbled. Not only was he physically intimidating, Wayne's neighbour was threatening in other ways. He had a 'hair-trigger' temper. His temper would erupt at the slightest provocation, and Wayne would have to endure a stream of foul language and threats of physical harm. Wayne was so stressed by his neighbour's behaviour that he would carefully check to see if his neighbour could be seen before leaving his house. He would then race to the car and drive away from his home. He would only attempt to do work in the garden when his neighbour was not at home. Wayne felt like his neighbour's whereabouts had become almost an obsession for him. Certainly, he felt that he couldn't do anything without making sure there was no risk of running into the bully who lived next door.*

Longer-term residents

People who have lived in their residence for a long period of time may develop a view that they have a greater say in how people in their neighbourhood should behave. Although having no greater rights that anyone else in their neighbourhood, they can believe the duration of their residence has given them the right to be the decision-makers. These people can be quite definite about what is acceptable for others and those things typically are the ones that will suit them.

> *When Anthony and Olivia moved into their new home, the older lady next door sat them down and told them how their neighbourhood worked. She had a list of things they were allowed to do and things that were prohibited. There were time restrictions on when they could do things. They were told that there were limits to how many guests they could invite to their home at any one time because of the 'parking pressure' visitors to the neighbourhood could cause. Anthony and Olivia were stunned and thought the demands being placed on them were ridiculous. Indeed, the list of dos and don'ts was generated by this neighbour and did not reflect any genuine regulations. However, when Anthony and Olivia spoke to other neighbours about the matter, they were surprised to find that others advised them to just go along with the demands. They told them their lives would be easier if they didn't cause a fuss and just did what they were told. The other neighbours told Anthony and Olivia that their neighbour had lived there longer than everyone else and expected them all to do what she wanted. They said she would never relax the 'rules' and it was simpler just to try to abide by them.*

Intimidators and bullies

There are some problematic neighbours who take advantage of or increase power imbalances. They intimidate and bully for the same reasons that threatening individuals and bullies engage in these types of behaviours. These people like the power they believe these types of behaviours give them. Also, the greater the bullying and intimidation, the less likely it is that the targeted neighbours will stand up to them.

> *Although no one in the street was prepared to say so in public, they all knew that the man who lived at No.46 was a bully. He seemed to take pleasure in upsetting those around him. If they met him on the footpath, he would walk down the middle so that they would have to step onto the road to get around him. He would stand in front of their homes when they were in their front yards, staring them down. This man did things that were threatening to others. He would drive his car down the middle of the street, forcing those coming towards him onto the curb. He would tailgate his neighbours if he was driving up behind them. He was trying to intimidate them, and it was working. His neighbours were intimidated. He thought he owned the street, and no one really told him otherwise.*

So, we have discussed the different types of problems people have with their neighbours. We have also identified that, in some of these cases, there exists an underlying power imbalance that advantages one person over another. Now let's consider what provokes or escalates a situation that develops to problematic proportions.

Provocations and escalations

We should take a moment to consider the ways in which neighbour disputes escalate and what provokes this. This is important because what starts out as a minor dispute can end up as a major conflict without you really knowing why that happened.

Demands

A dispute between neighbours typically starts with a demand. 'Don't do that.' 'Do more of this.' The person who makes the demand feels justified in doing so. However, the other person tends to react to this demand as an unwanted intrusion in their lives and a disregard for their right to live their life the way they want.

> *Ethan's property boundary was delineated by a creek that ran between his property and the property next door. Ethan's neighbour 'declared' that the land on either side of the creek should be 'shared space'. Ethan never agreed to this, but as he thought it would never become a problem, he did not openly reject what the neighbour had said. Ethan maintained the area that was his property, but his neighbour did nothing to maintain his side of the 'shared space'. Without significantly impacting the native vegetation in the area, Ethan cleared some noxious weeds that had been growing in the area and created a small walkway near the creek on his land so that he could easily enjoy that part of his property without damaging the surrounding flora. He planted some additional native shrubs to make the area attractive to local wildlife. Unexpectedly, from Ethan's point of view, the neighbour's anger erupted. The neighbour raised his voice and told Ethan he had no right to change the 'shared space'. He demanded that Ethan revert the small area to the way it was originally.*

Ignoring reasonable expectations

Often, we have an expectation that others will act fairly and reasonably if we just explain to them our point of view. To you, your point of view makes sense. It is quite confronting when you experience the rejection of what you see as reasonable. We will be discussing expectations of fairness later in this workbook.

> *Ethan tried to explain to his neighbour that he had not damaged the area in any way. He told his neighbour he had removed some plants that had been classified as weeds and replaced them with native plants that were indigenous to the area. To enjoy the area, he created a pathway between the shrubs that would allow him to walk among them without damaging them, but he had not otherwise introduced any materials that did not belong there. Ethan also pointed out that he had only done some gardening on his own property, and it had not impacted his neighbour's property in any way. Ethan had expected that his neighbour would calm down and see that he had not done anything harmful to the area and was entitled to do what he had done on his own property. He was surprised when his neighbour refused to change his attitude towards the matter and again demanded that Ethan 'repair the damage' he had done.*

Refusing to compromise

Disagreements exist when one person holds a view that is different from the other person's view. Both parties think they are right. However, even if this was the case, a dispute could easily be resolved if both parties were willing to compromise. A problem arises when one or both parties refuse to compromise. We will be discussing this issue later in this workbook. Here, it is worth saying that when a compromise is not considered, this is because both participants in the dispute think the other person should be the one who changes their mind and their behaviour.

> *In an effort to resolve the dispute, Ethan suggested he could plant out the pathway. He reasoned that this would only require a couple of extra plants, and the area would then grow like a native forest without the weeds he removed. But his neighbour refused to budge. He continued to insist that the area be restored to its original state and made it clear he would settle for nothing less than that.*

A change in attitude

When a conflict develops, it often does not remain stable. Instead, it tends to escalate. The disagreement about one issue starts to influence how you view other issues. For example, it is hard to separate your unhappiness with regard to your interactions with your neighbour about a dispute from your general feelings about the neighbour. You start to view all things your neighbour does in a more negative way than you would if the dispute did not occur. Even if you are not friendly with your neighbour, your view can shift from a neutral position (e.g., not having any particular view of your neighbour's behaviour) to a negative position that encompasses most or all aspects of the neighbour's behaviour.

> *Ethan had now had enough of his neighbour's behaviour. Despite previously being on quite friendly terms, Ethan now considered his neighbour to be a fool. He could not understand how anyone would think that a mess of weeds was preferable to an area of native plants. Ethan started to list in his mind all the things his neighbour had done over the years that had annoyed him. He now saw these things as much worse than he felt they were at the time they were done. Ethan decided he didn't like him as a person. He was now furious that his neighbour had the audacity to declare any part of Ethan's property 'shared space'.*

An escalation of conflict

Although we will be addressing this issue when we discuss managing your anger, it is worth saying here that conflicts with neighbours can escalate out of control. One neighbour kicks off the conflict, you then react, they up the ante, you become enraged, they push harder... you can see how this works. This occurs because of how human beings interact with each other in situations characterised by heightened emotional states. There is a pattern of increasing emotional arousal, with each participant feeding off the other's emotional state during the interaction. So, something that starts out as a problem that could be easily resolved if both participants chose to do that ends up escalating to a neighbourhood 'war'.

> *With the neighbour's latest demand to 'rehabilitate' the area, Ethan told his neighbour that the offer to change the area was no longer available and that he would do whatever he wanted on his own property. His neighbour threatened legal action. Ethan responded by placing rocks along either side of the short walkway so that it was clearly delineated. His neighbour came onto Ethan's property and pulled out a few of the native plants Ethan had added to the area, leaving them lying on the ground. Ethan reported the neighbour to the police for trespassing and destroying property.*

Your contribution to the escalation

It is a difficult thing to accept when you are having a disagreement with someone that you might be contributing to the problem, at least in part. Your contribution might be the way you react to the provocations of another person, or it may be by way of an omission when you do not do something that would help resolve the problem. The understanding that you might contribute to the escalation is not to say that you are automatically the one responsible for the issue arising, far from it. However, how you choose to react to a dispute with a neighbour may influence whether or not the conflict escalates. We will learn more about this later in this workbook.

> *Ethan had an uncomfortable feeling about the whole matter. Although he felt angry with his neighbour, he couldn't see where this conflict was going to end. He realised that by provoking his neighbour by marking the pathway with rocks on either side and by phoning the police, the matter was just continuing to escalate. But Ethan found the thought of stepping away from the conflict to be unpalatable. He believed he was in the right and that standing down would allow his neighbour to 'win'. Ethan was determined not to let that happen.*

It is easy for things to escalate to a point that could not have been anticipated at the outset of the dispute. With each step in the escalation, you move further and further away from an easy resolution. Although it is reasonable to stand up for your rights, doing so in an atmosphere of civility is preferable.

Maintaining civility and understanding your rights

The expectations people have about the nature of their relationship with their neighbours differ between people. Some want active involvement and close personal relationships. Some want amiable engagement, such as waving to each other in passing. Others want their privacy and prefer not to know their neighbours. In the context of this, it can be difficult to know what you are trying to achieve in your relationship with your neighbours.

Goal of keeping the peace

Some neighbours are very friendly. They are in and out of each other's homes. They have street parties, and they give each other the keys to their properties. It is nice if this happens as long as it is what people want. However, it is not necessary to have this level of engagement with your neighbours. It is acceptable to live your life separately from your neighbours. You should be able to have your privacy respected if this is your preference.

Even if you choose not to engage with your neighbours, there is a fundamental consideration that needs to be addressed. Your neighbourhood will be a more liveable and comfortable one if you and your neighbours keep the peace. By this, we mean that you will live in a more workable neighbourhood where people live in proximity to others if your baseline position is that the peace should be kept. We are referring here to a value you hold, which is that a peaceful neighbour is desirable.

It is easier to maintain this value of keeping the peace if your actions are guided by a need for civility. This refers to an intention to act in a courteous and polite manner, as demonstrated by your actions and what you say. Of course, the obligation you might take on to act in a civil manner may not be reciprocated by others. We will be discussing ways to deal with this later in this workbook.

Standing up for your rights

A point to be made here is that a decision to act in a civil manner in an effort to achieve your goal of keeping the peace does not stop you from standing up for your rights. It does not require that you allow a more aggressive neighbour to 'walk all over you'. Later in this workbook, we will introduce you to the notion of assertiveness and how it can help you deal with neighbourhood disputes. Assertiveness refers to the action of standing up for your rights without trampling all over the rights of others.

The mistake that people make is that, when trying to stand up for their rights, they make mistaken assumptions that they must do this forcefully and in an aggressive manner. Alternatively, a person may not stand up for their rights and, to their detriment, allow others to do as they wish in cases where it is contrary to what they need. Later, you will learn ways to stand up for your rights.

Understanding your rights

We are often not clear about our rights, particularly those that relate to our ability to take charge of our lives. Let's look at some of the mistaken assumptions we make that may be related to your current situation and your legitimate rights. We will also consider how holding these mistaken assumptions might affect how you react when you are involved in a dispute with a neighbour and how abandoning the mistaken assumption may improve your situation. Your rights do not only relate to your civil or legal rights but also to other, more personal rights.

Table 1: Mistaken assumptions, their consequences and your legitimate rights.

Mistaken assumption	*It is selfish to put your needs before the needs of others.*
Consequence	You may end up allowing a neighbour to behave in ways that significantly impact you and negatively influence the quality of your life. For example, Joanne thought it would be selfish to ask her neighbours to quiet down after 10 pm despite the fact that her work hours started at 7 am and she needed to get some sleep to be able to manage her workday.
Legitimate right	You have a right to put yourself first some of the time.
Outcome	Understanding your rights may allow you to speak up and try to find a solution to a problem that would otherwise be left unresolved. At the very least, you would be giving your neighbour a chance to act reasonably. They cannot do this if they do not know there is a problem.
Mistaken assumption	*You shouldn't take up other's valuable time with your own problems.*
Consequence	No one knows you need help unless you say so. If you do not say anything, you are unlikely to receive the support and help you might need. For example, Justin thought his friends should not have to listen to him complain about the trouble he was having with his neighbour. His friends were unaware that he was having a problem.
Legitimate right	You have a right to ask for help or emotional support.

Outcome	The people who care about you will understand you need help and offer it to you if they are able if you speak up and tell them what is going on. They may be able to give you some good advice if they know what is happening to you.
Mistaken assumption	*People don't want to hear that you feel bad, so keep it to yourself.*
Consequence	Your feelings are never expressed, and you end up feeling bottled up and isolated. For example, Jonas had never felt more stressed in his life… that he could remember. This was because he felt he was under a relentless attack from an aggressive neighbour. But when he was around his friends, Jonas acted like his normal, cheerful self. He felt he did not have the right to impose his stressed state on others.
Legitimate right	You have a right to feel and express pain.
Outcome	You will be able to feel some relief by sharing how you feel. Your emotional pain is not harmful to others who care about you. Friendships should be equal and reciprocal in that you should support your friends, and they should support you in times of distress. Accepting that people may be concerned about you, frees you to express how you are feeling and allows your friends to do something for you at a time when it probably seems to them there is little they can do to make things better.
Mistaken assumption	*When someone takes the time to give you advice, you should take it seriously.*
Consequence	You may be overwhelmed by people who are telling you what you should do. Unfortunately, the advice from one person can conflict with the advice from another, which only increases your confusion. For example, Andrea received a lot of conflicting advice about how to handle the escalating situation with her neighbour. Some of the advice-givers were very insistent that she do as they suggested, escalate the matter, and take civil action against the neighbour.
Legitimate right	You have a right to ignore the advice of others.

Outcome	You will come to realise that the advice people give you is only their opinion and the final decision will be yours to make. You should not then feel pressured to do what others demand or expect if it contradicts with what you need.
Mistaken assumption	*You should always try to accommodate others. If you don't, they won't be there when you need them.*
Consequence	You will be so busy thinking about what others need that you will have no opportunity to consider your own needs. Elizabeth's neighbour objected to Elizabeth's grandchildren playing outside at her home. The neighbour said it was not a 'children's neighbourhood' and Elizabeth needed to respect that. Elizabeth did not want to off-side the neighbour, so she kept the children inside and would not allow them to play in the yard. The children became less inclined to visit their grandmother.
Legitimate right	You have a right to say no to what is being asked of you.
Outcome	You are the person who decides how you wish to conduct yourself. If something is not prohibited and, as far as you can determine, any reasonable person would see it as acceptable, you can just politely refuse the request.
Mistaken assumption	*Don't be anti-social. People are going to think you don't like them if you say you'd rather be alone instead of with them.*
Consequence	If you give in to the efforts on your neighbour's part to intrude into your personal space and insist on spending time with you, you can find yourself in a situation where your preference to be alone is being disregarded. For example, Christine preferred her own company. She had lots of hobbies that she enjoyed and took up her time. She had a neighbour who would drop in for a cup of coffee and chat every day. Christine thought she had to tolerate these visits despite them feeling like a real intrusion.

Legitimate right	You have a right to be alone, even if others would prefer your company.
Outcome	By understanding you have a right to time to yourself, you may be able to strike a good balance between being around others and being alone to live your life the way you prefer by speaking up and making your needs known.
Mistaken assumption	*You should have a good reason for what you feel and do.*
Consequence	You waste energy thinking about how you are presenting yourself to others and worrying about what they think about you. For example, Wendy did not use her driveway as she did not have a car. Her neighbours had taken it upon themselves to park in her driveway. She asked them not to do so. Her neighbours demanded she explain why she should be upset about them using her driveway considering she did not use it.
Legitimate right	You have a right not to have to justify yourself to others.
Outcome	You should be able to tell people what you want to have happen on your own property without having to justify yourself for making the decision you have made. Although you may choose to offer an explanation, you have no real obligation to do so, especially in cases where others may choose to do the same as you if they were in your position. For example, your neighbours may very well object if you chose to park in their driveway.
Mistaken assumption	*When someone is in trouble, you should help them.*
Consequence	This may cause you to ignore your own needs in favour of the needs of others. This can result in your needs never being met. For example, Walter was having trouble with the unruly children of the single mother who lived next door. They were throwing things at his house and trampling over his garden. But Walter did not want to say anything because he knew their mother was struggling and he did not want to burden her further by asking her to discipline her children.
Legitimate right	You have a right not to take responsibility for someone else's problem.

Outcome	There are times in life when your needs exceed the needs of others, even if they are facing problems of their own. Understanding this may free you to focus on your own needs without worrying about the needs of others. For example, Walter's need to not have his property damaged probably exceeds his neighbour's right to ignore parenting responsibilities.
Mistaken assumption	*It is not nice to put people off. If questioned, give an answer.*
Consequence	Believing this, you may feel pressured to discuss things you do not want to discuss at times when you are not feeling able to discuss them. For example, Trudy's neighbour wanted the fence between their properties replaced… not because it needed replacing but because the neighbour wanted a particular type of fence that was aesthetically pleasing but expensive. The neighbour told Trudy she would have to pay half the cost. Trudy needed to consider the financial implications of agreeing to replace the fence. However, Trudy felt pressured to say yes because her neighbours were so insistent that she agree to their plan.
Legitimate right	You have a right to choose not to respond to a situation.
Outcome	Just because someone wants something to happen and for it to happen immediately does not mean you have to agree. You have a right to consider all aspects of your decision before making it. If there is no legal or regulatory reason for doing what is being asked of you, you can take your time to decide.

In many cases, asserting your legitimate rights is largely a matter of you accepting that these rights are legitimate and then calmly acting on that understanding. However, in other cases, you will be required to respond to a demand from someone else. We will cover how to assert your rights in an upcoming section of this workbook.

The trap of anticipating wrongdoing

As previously mentioned, we can start to view all actions of another person negatively when we are engaged in a dispute with them. This can lead to an escalation of conflict that does not help the situation. We can then begin to expect that the neighbour is going to behave badly before they actually do so.

Avoiding expectations of wrongdoing

There are many times we assume we know what is going to happen even when we actually cannot be certain. We may believe that a person will behave incorrectly or badly because, in our opinion, they have done so in the past. We may expect that a person will behave badly because we have formed a view that they are not of good character... or they are just hard to get along with... or we believe that nothing ever goes your way.

Although we may make good guesses about how people will respond, they are still just guesses. However, there is a greater likelihood of a negative outcome in any interaction with another person if you have expectations of wrongdoing. Having these expectations will also cause you to give up trying to resolve a problem because you feel certain there is no point and the person you are in dispute with is destined to behave badly.

Felicity and John had had a run-in with their neighbour over a fence replacement. They had wanted to increase the height of the fence between their property and the neighbour's property. The proposed height of the fence was considerable and above that allowed by local government regulations. They applied for an exemption. The reason they wanted to increase the height of the fence was so that they could not see into their neighbour's yard when they were in their upstairs bedroom. The visibility into other people's yards on the other boundaries was influenced by mature trees that grew there. From the neighbour's yard, all that could be seen if someone chose to look up was the ceiling of the bedroom. So, the heightened fence was solely for the benefit of Felicity and John. The problem was that the higher fence was going to impact significantly the sun shining into the neighbour's yard in the afternoons. The neighbour lodged an objection to the exemption application and Felicity and John were refused permission to increase the fence height that was proposed to be higher than allowed. Now, Felicity and John wanted to build a little summer house in the back corner, away from the boundary with the neighbours who objected to the fence. The proposed summer house would have no impact on the neighbouring property whatsoever. Nevertheless, Felicity and John were convinced that their neighbour would object to the plan to build the summer house. Their hostility towards their neighbour increased despite the neighbours knowing nothing about the proposed plan and despite the likelihood that they would not object to the construction of the summer house.

Incorrect interpretations

Expecting people to do the wrong thing tends to influence our interpretation of other people's behaviour. We will filter out signs that things are all right and focus only on the information that supports our belief that they are going to do something wrong. With this expectation that people will do the wrong thing all the time, we misinterpret even quite neutral actions that are not associated with any wrongdoing.

> *Felicity and John's attitude towards their neighbour deteriorated. They had already been disappointed by the rejection of the exemption application for the fence, and they blamed the neighbour for their disappointment. Felicity and John started to see their neighbour in a different way. When the neighbours put in a small vegetable patch, Felicity and John were critical of the decision. They were unhappy that their neighbour thought it was all right to make changes to their garden despite preventing Felicity and John from making changes to theirs... even though the two projects were very different. Felicity started referring to her neighbour as 'selfish'. Things the neighbour had always done that had never bothered Felicity and John before now were problematic for them. They were unhappy when their neighbour sat outside on their back deck, chatting with a friend. They viewed the noise created by the quiet chat to be intrusive. In fact, Felicity and John now had a list of complaints about their neighbour, including that they were too unreasonable to let them construct a summer house... even though they were never asked their opinion on the matter.*

Aggravation of your emotional state

This tendency to expect people to do the wrong thing and incorrect interpretations of events in ways that support your point of view can have a detrimental influence on your emotional state. You can become riled up and upset, even in the absence of any wrongdoing. This aggravated or heightened emotional state, in turn, will increase the tendency to predict poor behaviour.

> *Felicity and John thought their neighbour was destroying their lives. Although they would have described themselves as easy going prior to the dispute with the neighbour over the fence, they no longer felt that way. In fact, they felt stressed much of the time. Just being aware of their neighbour's proximity was enough to rile them. If they heard the neighbour start their car or saw them arrive home from work, their stress level would increase. Felicity and John were both having trouble sleeping, and they would talk into the night about how badly they had been treated by their neighbour. Now, everything the neighbour did aggravated and irritated them. They just 'knew' they were going to have problems with the neighbour in the future. Interestingly, though, the neighbour had no idea they felt like this or that there was a problem at all.*

We will discuss this notion of expecting poor behaviour and how our thoughts can influence how we feel and what we choose to do later in this workbook. For now, we need to learn more about understanding difficult neighbours and your reaction to them.

Understanding individual differences

There is an important aspect of learning how to cope with difficult neighbours that we need to consider. That is, we need to understand the nature and extent of individual differences between people and how they affect the way a person approaches a conflict.

No matter who you are, you generally think you are on the side of 'right', and the person with whom you have a dispute is on the side of 'wrong'. The person who you believe to be in the wrong thinks they are right and you are wrong. Pick any disagreement in any aspect of your life, and you will find this to be almost always true.

The extent to which you believe the 'rightness' of your perspective is difficult to shift. This is true even if you can see that there are two sides to every story when you are observing other people's disagreements and disputes.

We bring our own perspectives to any disagreement in which we are involved. The way we look at the disagreement is influenced by aspects of ourselves. Indeed, it is the case that conflict exists because we view things differently. Our views are influenced by factors such as our emotional state, our moods, our personality characteristics and our life experiences.

In understanding why people have their own perspectives about a conflict when you believe the 'right' view is obvious, consideration should be given to one feature of individuals that will help make sense of these differences.

Your values versus the values of others

Your values are the beliefs you hold and the principles that guide you. They are the aspects of the way you look at the world and understand how it works that help you make sense of how you should be acting and what you stand for. Your values should help you prioritise the things that are important to you. They should guide your decision-making. They should influence how you behave towards other people.

Value systems differ between people. What you find important in your life might not be the same as what others may view as important. Even if it is the case that you hold traditional values similar to the values of lots of other people, others may hold more unconventional values.

> *Penelope had clear views about what was important in life. She liked to help others and to be a good neighbour. She was involved in community groups. She liked to keep her garden looking nice so that her property enhanced the streetscape. Although her children were grown, she had raised them well. She had set some strict rules about their behaviour so that they grew up to be 'good citizens'. Penelope was a warm person who helped people when they needed some assistance.*
>
> *Gwyneth was Penelope's neighbour. She was a very different person to Penelope. Gwyneth wasn't really interested in community groups or being an involved neighbour. She liked her garden looking wild and thought life was too short to have lawns to mow. Gwyneth had young children, and she liked to describe them as 'free range'. She let them play in their quiet street, and the children could often be seen riding their bikes on the road or playing with their toys on the footpath. Her children occasionally did not attend school. Gwyneth liked to live her life on a 'wait and see' basis rather than planning for a future that she believed she might want to change as time went on. Although Gwyneth wasn't particularly interested in what Penelope was doing, Penelope was bothered by and didn't understand Gwyneth's approach to life.*

Whose value system is right?

There is no such thing as a 'correct' value system as such. There may be values that can be seen as desirable and promote respect, compassion, and law-abiding behaviour. Other values may be characterised by self-sufficiency, self-promotion and achievement. Still others may focus on self-indulgence, or kindness, or environmental concern. Some value systems promote personal wellbeing or the wellbeing of others. Other value systems can lead to destructive choices.

The particular combination of values you hold influences your view of the world. Your values help you make sense of your world. The combination of values held by others influences their views of the world and helps them make sense of their world.

The values we hold develop as a result of our experiences throughout life, starting in childhood, and from our experience of the environment in which we live. Our values and beliefs can change over time because we continue to experience the events and influences in our lives. It is obvious, then, that some people are going to have good influences, and their value systems are more likely to be healthy. Others will have poor life experiences, and their value systems may well reflect those influences.

So, rather than being right or wrong, a person's values can best be understood as healthy and helpful or unhealthy and not helpful. The influence on a person's life will be determined by the values that develop as a function of life experiences.

You can make a judgement about the relative merits of your value system relative to someone else's. You may not have had the same life experiences as others or similar influences on your life. For example, the impact of people who guide and mentor you throughout your life may have affected you differently from other people. By considering these factors, you might be able to begin to understand why you do not always see things the same way as a neighbour.

> *It would be fair to say that Penelope and Gwyneth didn't understand each other. On Gwyneth's part, she had no real interest in what Penelope was doing or how she chose to live her life. On Penelope's part, she just couldn't understand why anyone would live their life in the way that Gwyneth chose. But there were things about each other they didn't know. Growing up, Penelope had lived in the same house throughout her childhood. Her parents had instilled in her the importance of having an organised life and a good life plan. They thought it was important to be good citizens and they encouraged Penelope to think of others besides herself and to go out of her way to help others, particularly if the cause was a good one. Although she had her own way of doing some things, the fundamental lessons Penelope's parents had taught her were used to guide her way through life. Gwyneth's childhood could not have been more different. Her parents were loving people, but their lives were more relaxed. They moved around a lot, preferring to go to places and do things that interested them in the moment. As a result, Gwyneth's schooling was a bit haphazard, and she never spent long in any of the many schools she attended. Gwyneth's parents encouraged her to put personal happiness above other considerations. Although they wanted her to be a good person and not harm others, they considered other people to be responsible for their own happiness and well-being.*

Traditional versus unconventional

One other matter that needs to be considered when we seek to understand the influences on the way we see the world that we have already mentioned is the issue of how your value system differs from others in terms of its traditional nature. Although there might be individual differences between the specific values a person holds, those values might be considered traditional in nature. These types of traditional values influence the choices people make in life. By traditional, we refer to long-standing views that are shared by many others in your society.

In contrast, others hold different values that are not traditional. These values can be understood to be unconventional. The choices that people make because of these values are less traditional and more unconventional.

The important point to make is that unconventional values are different from traditional values, but they are not automatically wrong as a result. It is just harder for a person with traditional values to understand the unconventional value holder's choices or, for that matter, for the unconventional value holder to understand the traditional value holder's choices.

> *Penelope lived a more traditional life than Gwyneth in lots of ways. She valued education and good citizenship. She had a life plan and worked hard to achieve the goals she set. Gwyneth's life was more unconventional. She was less diligent about the education of her children, believing they would be fine in the future even if they had the occasional day off because of their life experiences rather than formal education. She valued a happy life for herself and her children over any commitment to others. Penelope thought Gwyneth was wrong in the way she was living her life. Gwyneth didn't really spend any time thinking about what Penelope thought of her.*

Adopting a non-judgmental stance

So, what should we learn from all of this discussion of value systems? The important point is that there are different influences on people that affect how they choose to conduct themselves. There are some value systems that are healthier than others because they help people to make better choices or allow their lives to be easier.

When it comes to neighbourhood disputes, there are a couple of things you might want to keep in mind. Firstly, it is easy to hold negative views about people on a fundamental level if their views seem different to yours. You start to see the person as 'all bad'. You are then likely to view everything they do as wrong.

Secondly, the result of this is that you then start to dislike the individual rather than disliking their behaviour. When this happens, it is hard to change this feeling in any dispute resolution process. It is hard to compromise with someone you see as the enemy.

> *One day, Penelope backed her car out of her driveway and ran over a bike that one of Gwyneth's children had left lying on the footpath. The mishap resulted in Penelope having a punctured tyre on her car, and the bike was destroyed and beyond repair. Penelope thought that problems such as this would not happen if Gwyneth would only act more responsibly. Disregarding the fact that children sometimes make mistakes and leave things lying around, even in families where they are not encouraged to do so, Penelope blamed Gwyneth's poor parenting. She formed the view that there was nothing that she and Gwyneth would ever see eye-to-eye about. Penelope decided she was in the right and that she was not going to tolerate the chaotic behaviour next door any longer.*

A lot of problems between neighbours are easier to resolve if you see them as events in time rather than a manifestation of a greater problem with an individual's character. It is preferable to adopt a non-judgmental position with regard to the value system of others that drives their behaviour and focus on what you need resolving rather than what character flaws need fixing. By all means, dislike the behaviour but try to avoid forming a view about the person.

What should I tolerate?

Sometimes, it is hard to know what you should be objecting to and what you should be tolerating. The fact that you might be irritated by someone's actions does not automatically make it something you should not have to tolerate. However, although it can be difficult to determine, there are some factors that can guide this decision.

Deliberate versus accidental provocations

A distinction needs to be made between actions that are done deliberately with the intention of causing you distress or harm and actions that are not malicious in intention. That is, some things may irritate you and accidentally provoke your upset feelings and unhappiness.

When you are feeling animosity towards another person, it is not always easy to have a clear idea of their intention. We tend to assume that the other person is deliberately doing something to annoy us. We will discuss this more later in this workbook when we talk about managing your anger in response to your neighbour's behaviour. For now, it is worth reminding you that it helps to try to think clearly about whether the neighbour's intention is to cause you trouble or whether they are living their life in the way they choose and that inadvertently upsets you.

> *Florence and her neighbour had a frosty relationship. There had been a couple of minor disagreements about some issues that had blown over in the end but had left some feelings of animosity. Things escalated one day when Florence became infuriated with her neighbour's behaviour. Florence had done some washing and was intending to hang it on the clothesline in her yard. It was a sunny day... a good day for washing. Over the fence, Florence's neighbour had been doing some gardening. She had raked up some leaf litter and had trimmed back some dead branches on a couple of small trees. Because there was no wind, the neighbour thought it was a good time to rake it all into a pile and set fire to the garden rubbish. Unfortunately, at about the same time, Florence hung out her washing. The smoke from the neighbour's fire drifted over the fence straight into the path of Florence's washing. Florence was furious and yelled at her neighbour. She accused her of deliberately lighting the fire to cause a problem for Florence. She wasn't prepared to listen to the neighbour's denial that she deliberately lit the fire to cause a problem. Florence just kept berating the neighbour and would not let the matter go.*

Learn what the law says

It is a good idea to know where you stand from a legal perspective. This may direct what action you take to rectify a problem. There are laws that govern what you can and cannot do with and on your own property, including how that might impact the safety and amenity of another person's property. By learning what the law says, you can make a decision about the way in which you would like a problem resolved. If there is no law prohibiting what the neighbour is doing, you may seek to negotiate a solution. If you are inadvertently acting in a way that is impinging on a neighbour's legal rights, you may wish to amend your behaviour to resolve a dispute.

Local government regulations

In addition to state-wide laws, there are also local government restrictions on your behaviour or what you do on your property. These regulations are readily accessible and can help you determine how best to resolve a problem. They also help you determine whether you have legitimate grounds for complaint.

Who to call for assistance

Knowing who to call for assistance with your problem with your neighbour can be confusing. To simplify the matter, if you can determine that your neighbour is breaking the law, the matter should be reported to the police, or you may seek legal advice. An example would be your neighbour trespassing on your property. If your neighbour disregards local government regulations, then a call should be made to your local council offices.

It should be simple. However, there is some overlap. The police can be called out for matters such as noise violations that relate to breaches of local government regulations.

Negotiated outcomes

When no laws have been broken or local government regulations breached, there are still opportunities to seek assistance if your neighbour disregards your request for change. There are often neighbour dispute resolution processes available for you to access if the need arises. This assistance might be provided by local government or accessed through private organisations.

Taking advantage of available avenues

If you feel you need outside help, the important point is to take advantage of the options available to you to resolve the dispute you have with a neighbour. What outside help you access should be determined by the nature of the problematic behaviour being demonstrated by the neighbour. That is, you need to determine whether the behaviour breaks the law, breaches local government regulations or should rightly be dealt with using neighbourhood dispute resolution options. By selecting the appropriate avenue, you can avoid being rejected when you seek help from the wrong source.

Notion of justice and injustice

As we have stated, some problematic behaviours by neighbours will break the law, some will breach local government regulations, and others will just be irritating without them being illegal. Interestingly, irrespective of their legality, you can still feel a sense of injustice if a neighbour's actions are negatively impacting you. Understanding these feelings of injustice will help you to manage your anger and more effectively resolve difficult disputes.

It is only fair…

We all have an idea of what we think is fair or unfair. We are often incorrect. Fairness refers to the impartiality of treatment of all people involved. Fairness requires a lack of favouritism and an absence of discrimination. However, we do not always use 'fairness' in these terms… although sometimes we do.

If you listen to people when they are talking about what they consider to be fair or unfair, you will hear people referring to something being fair if it works out in their favour, if they get something in return for something they have done, or if other people 'see sense' and agree with them.

Probably the most common misuse of the term is when you expect someone to reciprocate in a manner you think is deserving. For example, in this view, a person is being fair if they recognise my contribution and give me something in return. However, if you think about it, this notion of fairness implies that there is some sort of universal record keeping of what people have done or have not done. No such record exists.

We also act as if there is some well-established standard of what is fair behaviour and what is not. No such standard has ever been established.

Further, we tend to think that people are being fair if they agree with us and unfair if they do not. However, if you think about it, it is not possible for one person to say what is 'fair' because others may have different views. Of course, none of these views actually directly relate to the true meaning of fairness.

Nonetheless, you will find the notion of fairness being raised in relation to neighbourhood disputes and difficult behaviour by neighbours. Some of the uses of this term will be closely related to its actual meaning.

> *Bob liked to think he was a good neighbour. He tried to be considerate of other people's needs and aware of the impact of his actions on others. He felt that if he behaved well, others should reciprocate. This is why Bob became angry when his neighbours bought themselves a new barbecue with a smoker attachment that they happily used... often. Bob always smelt food cooking, and sometimes, when the breeze was blowing in the wrong direction, smoke would drift into Bob's yard. Bob complained bitterly to his wife. She said people were allowed to barbecue on their own property, but Bob said it wasn't fair. He said he wouldn't do that to them, so they shouldn't do that to him.*

Feeling of injustice

When you feel that things are unfair, you often are referring to feelings of injustice. A sense of injustice can evoke a strongly negative emotional state. It makes us feel angry and frustrated. It can also make us feel helpless. It can also trigger a strong desire for revenge.

Interestingly, justice in a legal sense can be removed from what we see as justice or injustice. If something is causing us to feel a sense of injustice, we believe there should be a law preventing others from doing what they are doing. Sometimes that is true, but sometimes it is not. Our sense of injustice seems to relate more to what we think should happen and what we think should not happen.

> *Bob's anger was based on what he saw as the injustice of it all. He thought he should not have to suffer so that someone else had the pleasure of barbecuing. Bob was convinced there must be rules about barbecuing, and he spent some time searching for regulations or laws that would prevent his neighbour from cooking outdoors. He was disappointed that he could not find any information that would give him a good foundation to force his neighbour to cease his barbecuing behaviour. Despite this lack of legal support for his position, Bob continued to feel a sense of injustice, and his anger did not abate.*

Assumptions underlying this feeling of injustice

When we experience a sense of injustice, we tend to feel angry. These angry feelings are based on a number of assumptions we make. These assumptions are as follows.

> When faced with what we see as injustice, we make the assumption that we have been wronged. Something has happened to us that should not have happened.

> We also believe that someone has done something to us. It was not just an accident or a miscalculation. We tend to think it was deliberate.

We also believe that the person who has done something to us should not have done what they did. We assume they could have chosen to do something other than what they did, but they did not make this better choice.

These assumptions feed our anger. Without these assumptions, we might feel disappointment that something has happened, but we would be less likely to feel angry.

> *Bob was overwhelmed by the sense of injustice and unfairness he felt about his neighbour's barbecuing behaviour. Despite his wife trying to reason with him that barbecuing was normal and accepted backyard behaviour, Bob felt that what was happening was wrong. In particular, he felt that his neighbour was targeting him. Bob personalised his neighbour's behaviour. He felt that it was a direct attack on him. He convinced himself that his neighbour's behaviour was deliberately meant to cause him distress. And Bob was absolutely certain that his neighbour should not be doing this. Bob believed his neighbour should not be barbecuing because of the degree of upset it was causing him. Bob's wife gave up trying to get him to see sense.*

A 'feeling' of injustice, in itself, does not determine whether a wrong has been committed. That feeling also does little other than make us angry and resentful and drives us to think of ways to exact revenge. It makes us believe that the other person needs to change their behaviour to rectify a problem situation. We think they need to stop doing what they are doing, and it is only 'fair' that they do so.

Interestingly, this thought process makes us feel more out of control than in control. Instead of going down this pathway, we need to consider ways to actually be more in control.

Who is in control?

Typically, people feel better when they feel more in control than when they feel that things are out of their control. Few people would argue about this point, especially in relation to conflict and disagreement. However, we do not often see where our control efforts are best directed. Rather than seeking personal control, we tend to look to others to change so that things can be the way we want them to be.

Believing others should change to meet our needs

In situations where conflict exists, such as in disputes with neighbours, we tend to believe that other people should change so that we can feel better about a situation. But how is that being in control? What happens if the other person refuses to change? Waiting for someone else to choose to change is surely the opposite of being in control. Waiting for someone else to change just sounds frustrating and often pointless. It seems to be a better idea to take control of how we are reacting to an event so that things could be better for us.

> *Diana sought the advice of a counsellor with experience in mediating neighbourhood disputes. She had been experiencing some difficulties with the behaviour of her neighbour. In particular, her neighbour had a hobby of creating things out of wood. Diana's neighbour had some electric tools and saws that they would use some of the time. The noise disturbed Diana. Her neighbour didn't work on their hobby all the time and only used the power tools intermittently. Also, the neighbour only used the tools for brief periods during daylight hours. However, Diana felt that any noise intrusion was too much. Diana had asked her neighbour to stop using the tools, but the neighbour declined to do so. As a result of not being able to resolve the issue, Diana sought some advice from the counsellor, believing that the counsellor would tell her how to make her neighbour do as she had asked. But Diana was surprised when the counsellor asked her what she could do to better manage her reaction to the neighbour's behaviour. Diana reiterated that she wanted advice on how to get the neighbour to stop doing what they were doing. The counsellor responded by asking Diana what she was going to do if the neighbour simply refused to stop doing what, in truth, they were allowed to do.*

Personal change feels like defeat

Why do we reject the idea that we should take control of a situation by changing the way we do things? We reject the idea of personal change because it feels like a defeat. It feels like we have lost, and the other person has won. However, taking personal control of a situation can be viewed in a different way. By making personal decisions about how you are going to conduct yourself, you are the person who is in control.

> *Diana struggled to let go of the idea that it was her neighbour who had to stop using power tools rather than Diana having to find ways to cope with the noise or find some other way of dealing with the intrusion. She felt that she was being controlled by the neighbour. Diana could not see that, by choosing to manage the situation, she would be the one who was taking control of her own situation. Diana didn't think it was fair that she was the one who had to change. The counsellor tried to explain that Diana was not giving up anything by managing the situation in ways that she could control. It was pointed out to Diana that by doing something herself, she was taking charge. By waiting and hoping the neighbour would stop using power tools, she was handing over control to the neighbour.*

Personal change is your strength

You certainly have more chance of achieving some control over a situation if you put yourself in charge of influencing the outcome. Being the person who influences the outcome puts you in a position of strength.

There is nothing 'unfair' about you doing your best to take charge of the pathway of your life. It seems like a passive response to a problem to wait for others to change their behaviour as the solution to a dispute. It is preferable to take the opportunity to act in ways that influence the behaviour of others to encourage them to change. We will examine various ways to take control later in this workbook.

Who will be the winner?

In most disputes, we assume there will be a winner and a loser. This adversarial stance assumes that someone is right and will prevail, and someone is wrong, and they will have to abandon what they have been doing or do the things they have not been doing but should be doing. However, have you considered taking a different perspective? Let's first consider the notion of a win-lose approach.

Choosing a win-lose approach

Choosing a win-lose approach pits you against an adversary. It makes the resolution of a dispute much more difficult to achieve. In a win-lose approach, there is no expectation of compromise. Rather, it is a 'win at all costs' approach. With this attitude, you are more likely to reject offers, discount the importance of compromise, and refuse to move away from your expected outcome.

> *Jenny was a competitive person, and she liked to win. So, when an issue arose with a neighbour about Jenny's proposed extension on her house, she was determined to make sure the objection the neighbour had about the encroachment of the extension on her property would not prevent Jenny from building the extension she wanted. Potential resolutions for the problem were suggested by planning officers, the builders and the neighbour, but Jenny rejected all of them. No matter how long it took, Jenny was determined to win. She would do whatever it took to make the neighbour stand down, and the planning officers accept her plans. This was despite the fact that it had been made plain to her that her planning application would not be accepted without the necessary changes because the objection by the neighbour was a valid one. As determined as Jenny was to win, so was the neighbour not to have the extension encroach on their property.*

Us-versus-them attitude

A win-lose approach encourages an us-versus-them stance. This fuels the sense of injustice you feel and encourages refusal to compromise. It causes you to blame others for your unhappiness, even when you could have acted differently to obtain a better outcome. An us-versus-them attitude aids the development of negative feelings and increases personal stress. Viewing people as 'enemies' is not very comfortable for you.

> *In her effort to win, Jenny started a war. Even though there was no actual relationship between Jenny's neighbour and the local government planning officers, Jenny responded to both as if they were acting together to challenge her. Rather than considering that what she was expecting to happen was not reasonable, she saw her neighbour and the planning officers as thwarting her ambitions to have what she wanted. She spoke about both parties in disparaging terms. She made a formal complaint about the planning officer, but she couldn't do the same about the neighbour. Instead, she started to make life for the neighbour difficult. She objected to everything the neighbour did. Her lawn mower was too loud. She blamed the neighbour for the wind blowing leaves into her yard. She fitted outdoor lighting that significantly impacted the neighbour's home. In effect, she treated the neighbour as her enemy. She saw the neighbour as the problem. What she failed to realise is that, in her determination to win and in treating her neighbour as the enemy, Jenny had become the problem neighbour.*

Choosing a win-win approach

A better approach is one that seeks a win-win outcome. An approach that seeks a win-win outcome is one that tries to obtain a good outcome for both parties. It is understandable that the negative feelings that develop in many disputes can make a win-win solution seem undesirable. However, there are advantages to a win-win approach.

> A win-win approach encourages both parties in the dispute to commit themselves to resolving a problem situation that might have arisen. It encourages participation in the process of resolution.

> Such an approach allows you to have a civil or working relationship in the future with the other party of the dispute. There tend to be fewer ongoing ill feelings if both parties gain something in the process of resolution. There is less likelihood of lingering resentment and hostility.

> A win-win solution is one that is likely to have longer standing effects. With both parties being happy with the outcome, there is less likelihood that either party will demand that the dispute is revisited.

> *At the outset of this dispute, Jenny was offered options that would have allowed for the extension of her house to be built. Her neighbour would still have had to have the extension built too close to the boundary for her liking, and Jenny would not have had the extension built in the way she preferred. However, with the neighbour being satisfied as long as the extension did not encroach onto her land and as long as Jenny was satisfied with an extension that, to a large degree but not entirely, was what she wanted, Jenny would have been able to have an extension built and maintain a reasonable relationship with her neighbour. Without the compromise, Jenny would not have permission to build her extension, and it was unlikely that her relationship with her neighbour could be salvaged.*

Seeing the advantage of a win-win approach will help you achieve good outcomes. We will be talking more about win-win solutions in our discussion about negotiation strategies later in this workbook. Adopting a win-win mentality in your approach to problem resolution will set you in good stead.

Managing your environment

From here, we have to consider what to do to better manage the situation you find yourself in. There will be things that you can do that are external to you and things you can do that require you to change how you think about and approach the problem and the actions you choose to take. We will also cover ways to manage your emotional reactions. Let's start by looking at the management of your home environment, which is so important to your well-being.

Protecting your space

To feel secure in your home and on your property, the goal is to create an environment that allows you to feel protected. Secure locks and external cameras can assist you to feel less vulnerable.

We should be able to feel comfortable in our own home and on our own property. You need to have an environment where you do not feel vulnerable and can be free of concern about intrusion. You need to feel safe from harm and protected from danger. Of course, not everyone has these things in their home but they are still desirable things to have available to you.

Physical barriers

When we think about protecting our personal space, we tend to focus on physical barriers that prevent intrusion. To a large extent, this is why many properties have fences. They act as a demarcation line beyond which no one should cross uninvited.

As a physical barrier, fences and gates are good at protecting your space and will act to protect you to some degree with regard to certain problem situations. Lattice on top of your fence with climbing plants, for example, can provide you with improved protection from things like intrusive neighbours with prying eyes.

Also, fitting blinds or filmy curtains that allow in light but prevent people from seeing into your home can make you feel more comfortable. Alternatively, there are ways to retrofit coatings on your window panes to make it impossible for people to see in while still allowing light into your home.

Wind and privacy screens can act to protect you from being observed and can give you a sense of privacy. Further, privacy can be achieved by clever garden planting.

The important point is that physical barriers can be used to prevent intrusion and make you feel safer. These can be introduced without significantly altering your home.

Psychological barriers

You may like to consider psychological barriers to create the type of environment in your home and on your property that would allow you to feel less vulnerable. Although physical barriers are designed to prevent people from entering your space, the goal of a psychological barrier is to make you feel less aware of the presence of a neighbour.

Plantings in your garden can create a sense of isolation, separating you from the properties around you. The aim would be to design your outdoor space to give the feel of an oasis that has nothing around it to intrude.

Within your home you can place furniture to face away from people walking past your home. The same can be done for outdoor furniture. By placing seating looking away from the neighbours you want to avoid, a sense of being separate from them is created.

As well as being a physical barrier, security fences can serve as a psychological barrier. The peace of mind you have from knowing that no one can enter your property uninvited can allow you to relax and enjoy your personal space.

Wearing headphones or earbuds and listening to music when you are outdoors can block intrusive noise. In addition, they can also act as a psychological barrier by creating a sense of separation from others and making it seem to others that you are less available.

Although physical and psychological barriers can help protect your space, they are not the only consideration. You can benefit from learning to maintain boundaries that people should not cross.

Maintaining boundaries

When talking about boundaries, we are not referring to fences or other physical boundaries. We are referring to the limits you set to avoid intrusion and interaction with your neighbours. Some people find it challenging to set limits on the extent to which others intrude into their lives, especially with determined neighbours. We will be talking more about assertiveness later in this workbook, but for now, let's consider this issue of setting limits.

Friendly or neutral approach

There is a difference between being 'friendly' and being 'friends'. By being friendly, we refer to you saying hello or nodding towards your neighbour if you happen to be at your mailboxes at the same time.

By maintaining a particular type of 'friendly' attitude, you are controlling the tone of your interactions with your neighbour. However, it also allows you to draw a line, beyond which you do not cross. That is, you can be friendly and limit your interaction to the wave or nod but make it clear that you have no interest in your interaction with them developing further.

A mildly friendly reaction to your neighbour's presence can also be disconcerting to them. If they are expecting hostility and are primed to react in an equally hostile manner, a mildly friendly gesture can throw the other person off balance and cut short the response to your presence they intended to demonstrate.

Even if you choose not to say a friendly hello, you can choose a neutral acknowledgement of the presence of your neighbour. Again, this allows you to set the limits on your interaction with your neighbour. By establishing a neutral position in tone of voice, posture and attitude, you are defining the interaction you have with your neighbour and exerting some control over how the interaction develops.

> *Suzanna had what she considered to be an odd neighbour. Whenever Suzanna saw her neighbour, she could hear the neighbour muttering negative comments about her. These comments were generally denigrating, giving Suzanna hurtful labels. The neighbour rarely engaged in an actual conversation with Suzanna. Because Suzanna liked to be outdoors and spent a lot of time tending her garden, she did tend to see her neighbour often. Her enjoyment of her garden was being undermined by the neighbour's nasty comments. Suzanna didn't want to be confrontational with her neighbour as she felt this would escalate things. However, she felt she should be doing something in response to her neighbour's behaviour. Suzanna decided to call out a cheery 'good morning' or 'good afternoon' whenever she heard her neighbour muttering about her and then just continue with whatever she was doing at the time. She thought that even if this did not alter her neighbour's behaviour, it would certainly make Suzanna feel better.*

Limit interactions

Both the friendly and the neutral exchanges with a neighbour allow you to limit your interaction with your neighbour. It is a fact that if you engage in unplanned discussions with hostile neighbours when you are feeling hostile toward them, the exchange is likely to escalate into an angry interaction that will end up causing you distress.

Also, by limiting your interactions with your neighbour, you are exerting control over the extent to which your neighbour can upset you. We will be talking more about how your actions can influence the actions of another person and how this happens later in the workbook. Here, we are suggesting that it should be up to you to determine the extent to which you choose to interact with neighbours in a general way. Your involvement in interactions should not be forced by a neighbour.

> *William felt he had to dodge his neighbour. He wanted to dodge her. As a result, he would try to avoid running into her. Unfortunately, William now felt he had to tip-toe around his own property so that he did not run into her. The problem was that if she saw him, William's neighbour would bail him up to complain about all his imaginary infringements of his neighbour's rules for good conduct. William would try to be polite and listen to what she had to say, but these interactions could be lengthy, and it was difficult for William to step away from them. Unfortunately, it seemed that when his neighbour had his attention, there was no end to the complaints. And that is why William was hiding from his neighbour. However, William decided that he didn't want to do that anymore. He also didn't want to engage in long interactions with her. Although William would not normally walk away from someone mid-conversation, he decided that he would end the conversation after an initial greeting. He decided that the best option was to say 'hello' but then physically move away from his neighbour. If necessary, he would explain that he had lots of things to do and couldn't stay to chat. William felt that this allowed him to control the conversation and to avoid having to hide from his*

> *neighbour. He understood that his neighbour might prefer to prolong the interaction, but William decided he would not engage in these conversations because he had not given consent for the interaction to take place. He came to understand that there was nothing holding him there beyond a misplaced sense of politeness.*

Focus on your own space

If you have to run into your neighbour because of the situation of your property or the fact that your mailboxes are close by, and you do not wish to interact with them, then your focus should be on your space or what you are doing.

The thing you want to avoid is hiding if you feel you are at risk of running into your neighbour, except in circumstances where there is a threat of physical harm from them. Otherwise, you should take ownership of your space and understand your right to go about your daily activities despite the fact that you live near a neighbour you are finding difficult.

> *Bonnie and her neighbour played cat-and-mouse. If Bonnie was in her front yard and her neighbour came outside, she would retreat to the backyard. If her neighbour moved to her backyard and would watch her over the fence, Bonnie would go indoors. She did this because Bonnie's neighbour liked to act in ways that intimidated her. She felt it was a game her neighbour played to see how much influence she could have over Bonnie. She realised that her neighbour enjoyed making Bonnie retreat from her. So, Bonnie made a decision to stop being chased around by her neighbour. Bonnie reasoned with herself that it was her outdoor space and she should demonstrate ownership of it. Instead of moving away from her neighbour, Bonnie decided to just go about her business and do what she intended to do. She was determined not to demonstrate any sign that the neighbour's behaviour was disturbing or intimidating. In fact, Bonnie decided to act as if the neighbour wasn't there. She figured that she had every right to enjoy her garden irrespective of her neighbour's odd behaviour. She hoped that she would get tired of Bonnie's failure to react and would give up the cat-and-mouse game.*

You will be surprised by the extent to which how you react will influence how others will respond. Next, we will learn why this occurs and how you can use it to manage a difficult situation with your neighbour.

Extinguishing behaviour: The world of learning theory

To understand how your actions can be used to influence how another person responds to you, we need to explore the nature and influence of reinforcement. The pattern of reinforcement you adopt, that is, the system of rewards you use or take away in response to another person's behaviour, can have a strong influence on how they act towards you.

Understanding learning theory

To understand how reinforcement works, we need to delve into how people learn. Although there are different types of learning theory to explain how people acquire new information, the type of learning theory we want to examine is known as behavioural learning theory.

This learning theory looks at the rewards and punishments that influence people's actions. In general, people tend to do more of the things that are associated with a reward and fewer of the things that are associated with punishment.

In what is known as classical conditioning, if you pair a neutral stimulus with a naturally occurring behaviour, the two things will become linked. The most commonly known example of this relates to Pavlov's dog experiment. Pavlov was a Russian scientist with expertise in experimental neurology and physiology. He paired ringing a bell with giving the dog food. After the association between these two things was established, the dog would salivate when Pavlov rang the bell because the dog expected to be fed. Not that we are suggesting you ring a bell and have your neighbour salivate.

Instead, we are looking at a different type of conditioning. It is referred to as operant conditioning. In the case of operant conditioning, rather than linking a neutral stimulus with a naturally occurring behaviour, associations are formed between a particular behaviour and the consequences of that behaviour. Learning happens when specific behaviours are followed by either a reward or a punishment.

A person is likely to engage in a behaviour more often if it is associated with a positive outcome for them. For example, a person may pat their dog frequently because it makes them feel happy and relaxed to do so. A person is likely to avoid engaging in a behaviour if it is associated with a negative outcome. For example, a person may avoid sticking their finger into boiling water because they learn it will burn.

Let's consider the nature of reinforcement and how it relates to poor neighbour behaviour before considering ways you can use this knowledge to manage difficult neighbour behaviour in some cases.

Reinforcement and rewards

People think they understand the language of reinforcement but they often make mistakes and, for example, assume that the term 'negative reinforcement' is the same thing as 'punishment'. It is worthwhile to take a moment to clarify the terms and what function the various forms of reinforcement serve.

Positive reinforcement refers to a positive reward happening as a consequence of engaging in a particular behaviour. To use the example of a neighbour yelling abuse at you whenever they see you, the positive reinforcement that person receives is your obvious upset, your scared look or you heading back indoors whenever they yell at you. For this type of difficult neighbour, it is pleasing for them to see your reaction because it makes them feel powerful and in control.

Punishment refers to a negative outcome happening as a consequence of engaging in a particular behaviour. To use an example, a person would be punished if they had to pay a hefty fine every time they yelled at you. Bearing in mind that this example is unlikely to ever happen, the fine would be the punishment for engaging in the behaviour. A person who yells at you would then be less likely to do so because of the punishing fine.

Negative reinforcement has a completely different meaning. A behaviour is negatively reinforced when that behaviour serves to end a difficult emotional state or a painful experience. For example, if an action on your part caused your neighbour to stop yelling at you, that action would be negatively reinforced because it would cause the anxious state that happens when you are yelled at to cease. This negative reinforcement would cause you to be encouraged to continue to engage in the action that so strongly influences your neighbour's difficult behaviour and, therefore, reduce your anxiety. So, if a neighbour yells, you ignore them, you feel better, so you are more inclined to ignore them in the future. The act of ignoring them is being negatively reinforced by the cessation of your upset emotional state.

There is one other term we need to introduce. The term **extinction** is used to describe a situation where a behaviour ceases to occur because the reinforcement it would normally receive is withdrawn. **Extinguishing** a behaviour does not require that you actively punish an unwanted behaviour. It can also occur if you simply remove the positive reinforcement the person who is engaging in the behaviour is receiving. Herein lies the key to you exerting influence over a neighbour's behaviour.

How to respond

A difficult neighbour might engage in a behaviour, such as yelling abuse at you because it is rewarded. The reward is your response. In many cases, if a person 'pushes your buttons', it becomes apparent that you are upset. You look upset, and you act upset, such as racing inside to get away from the abuser. For someone who is trying to upset you, your reaction is rewarding for them. They keep doing the same behaviour over and over because you react in the same way every time.

The key to influencing the neighbour's behaviour that is unwanted and unwarranted, such as them yelling at you, is to withdraw the response that is rewarding. This would involve you responding in a neutral way to their actions. You just act as if you are unaware of what they are doing. The more you do this, the more the person doing the yelling learns that this type of behaviour simply does not evoke the same rewards it used to produce. Over time, the behaviour will be extinguished because there is no point in them doing it.

It sounds straightforward, but it is hard to do. This is because you become upset when your neighbour yells at you because it is genuinely upsetting to be yelled at. It is worth remembering here that, in the beginning, the goal is to *act* like you are not upset and not necessarily to stop being upset.

Now, you might say that it is embarrassing to be yelled at where other neighbours might see and hear what is going on. We should point out that, in general, when someone is yelling, the crowds tend to look at the person doing the yelling and not at the person being yelled at. Even if they glance in your direction, the attention of the crowd is drawn back to the person causing all the fuss. If anyone should be embarrassed, it should be the person who is yelling. Who would you look at if someone was yelling in the supermarket? You might glance around to see what is happening, but your attention would be drawn back to the person who is yelling.

> *Jocelyn spent as little time in the front of her house as she could manage. She tended to the garden when she had to and would collect the mail but would otherwise avoid spending any time there. This is because whenever she went out in front of her house, the woman who lived across the street would yell abuse at Jocelyn. She would call her names and use foul language. The neighbour would sit on her porch and keep watch over the neighbourhood, so it was hard for Jocelyn to avoid her. It was clear to Jocelyn that her neighbour enjoyed the effect she had on her. When Jocelyn would race back indoors, her neighbour would laugh out loud and provide a commentary on what Jocelyn was doing. As far as Jocelyn could determine, she was the neighbour's only target. She knew she had not done anything to aggravate the neighbour and assumed that she was the target because she lived in the neighbour's direct line of sight. The neighbour's behaviour always embarrassed Jocelyn. She wondered what the other neighbours were thinking about her. She was concerned that they would be thinking that she had done something to provoke it. However, Jocelyn got to the point where she had had enough. Rather than racing inside and trying to avoid the neighbour, Jocelyn decided to ignore her. She told her friend that she was starting a campaign of 'pointedly ignoring' her neighbour. After making that decision, Jocelyn would slowly wander to the mailbox, checking out her garden on the way. She would stand by her mailbox and go through the mail she had collected. She sat on her front doorstep with a good book and a cool drink. She replanted a garden bed at the front of the house. She did these things*

> *even when abuse was flung in her direction. Jocelyn had started her campaign to remove the reward her neighbour was receiving for her verbal abuse. She was hopeful that her neighbour would get tired of yelling if there didn't seem to be a purpose for doing it.*

Expecting escalation

Ah, but if only it was that easy. There is something that is likely to occur when you first implement your strategy to extinguish a behaviour by withdrawing the reinforcement that is maintaining the behaviour. That is, using our example, the person who is yelling at you is likely to react in a particular way to your initial withdrawal of the rewards they were receiving (you demonstrating you are upset).

In fact, what they are likely to do is to escalate their behaviour. Initially, they will try harder to elicit the response they are seeking. You have to be ready for this to occur. They will try harder to elicit the response because they have noticed that their actions are not working to make you upset in the way that they had previously. So, in effect, the escalation of their behaviour is a sign that your strategy is working.

There is a really important thing you have to do when you are confronted with this escalation. You need to hold your nerve or your ground or whatever it is you are holding. Do not allow this escalation to cause you to revert to demonstrating how upset you are. If you do buckle under the extra pressure, your neighbour learns that the way to elicit a response from you is to just try harder. Next time, they will not bother just yelling at you a little bit. They will yell at you a lot. This is because if you give in and become upset, they have learned what it now takes to get the reaction from you that they want.

We know that this sounds like a hard thing to do. You did not like being yelled at to a moderate degree, and you definitely would not like it if they yelled more. The important thing to remember here is that this escalation will not last forever if you just remain strong and refuse to reinforce the neighbour's behaviour with the reaction from you that they want. This is because the removal of the reward for their behaviour will eventually make their action not worthwhile. What is the point of yelling if no one is reacting to their behaviour? Remove their audience because there is no point carrying on if they have no one paying attention.

One way to help you deal with the short-term escalation of the troublesome behaviour is to take an imaginary step back from your involvement in the neighbour's actions. This is not about you and the neighbour. It is about the neighbour's behaviour. The best way to manage this is to take what is termed a 'spectator role' or an 'observer role'. Simply observe their behaviour for what it is. You can be aware of it happening without it impacting you in an immediate sense. You might say to yourself, "Isn't it interesting that they are doing that?" or "What a strange sort of behaviour for someone to engage in".

> *Jocelyn's nerve was tested after implementing her plan. Her 'ignoring' actions seemed to infuriate the neighbour, and the verbal abuse grew louder and more prolonged. But after so long being intimidated by this person, Jocelyn was determined not to buckle under the increased abuse. In fact, she did the opposite of what the neighbour wanted her to do. When the verbal abuse got louder, Jocelyn stayed sitting on her front step, reading her book for even longer. She invited her friend around to sit with her on the front step and have a chat. She started other gardening projects in her front yard. Jocelyn didn't like the abuse any less than she had previously, but she was tired of being intimidated by someone who couldn't seem to control their own appalling behaviour. For Jocelyn, ignoring the abuse was not the same thing as not hearing it. Nonetheless, she persisted with her plan of 'deliberate ignoring'. And then something happened. The verbal abuse became less frequent, or the neighbour would yell something briefly but then just glare at Jocelyn. This was followed by a quick burst of abuse followed by the neighbour going back inside her own home. Jocelyn was certain her plan had worked when it became apparent that the neighbour wasn't spending her time watching over the neighbourhood and waiting for Jocelyn to appear. In fact, Jocelyn hardly saw her anymore.*

Perseverance is the key

The key to success of this technique is perseverance. As stated, if you give in things will not revert to how they were before but will be worse because your neighbour has learned what it takes to get the result they want.

By persevering with your plan to withdraw the reward for your neighbour's behaviour, that behaviour will become 'extinct'. That is, the neighbour should stop doing what they were doing if the reward is withdrawn. Of course, that would not stop them adopting some other behaviour but if that new behaviour is managed in the same way then the chances are that, over time, the neighbour will discontinue these types of actions.

Of course, this will not solve all types of difficult behaviours by neighbours or resolve other types of neighbourhood disputes. We need to look at other options that are available for you to use. As part of your plan to manage the situation with your neighbour, it is a good idea to consider ways to manage the stress you feel when confronted with these types of problems.

Regulating your emotions

Undoubtedly, difficult interactions with neighbours are upsetting. This is true because otherwise, you would not see these interactions as difficult. Of course, they are upsetting, and they can have a significant impact on your emotional wellbeing. Let's have a look at what happens when you become upset and what you can do to feel better.

Primary and secondary emotions

Emotions are the reactions you have to the things that happen to you or the things you think about. When something good is happening, you will feel pleasurable emotions, and you will respond positively to your situation. When something bad is happening, you will experience distressing emotions, and you will view your situation negatively.

Human beings can experience a full range of emotional responses, from strongly negative to strongly positive. We are complex creatures with the capacity to experience a range of emotions as a result of any one event. Sometimes, this can be overwhelming. It then makes sense to be able to regulate your emotions so that the emotional state you are in does not overwhelm you.

Let's consider how we react emotionally. Initially, when something happens, we experience an emotional response. These initial responses are referred to as *primary emotions*. They are the reactions we have to our experiences.

However, as we are complex individuals, we can then develop an emotional reaction to our initial emotional reaction. These emotions are referred to as *secondary emotions*. Secondary emotions are the feelings we have about our feelings. Let's consider an example. You are travelling in a car with a friend, and you are listening to the news on the radio. A sad news item comes on, and you unexpectedly burst into tears. Then, you feel embarrassed that you felt so upset and cried in front of your friend. The upset feeling you experienced about the news item was your primary emotion. It was your initial reaction to what was happening. The embarrassment you felt was your secondary emotion. This was the feeling you had in response to your primary emotion.

Our secondary emotions can become quite complex. Consider the following example.

Example of complex emotions	
What happened?	*I tried to explain to my neighbour that their music was causing a problem because I am a shift worker and I regularly have to sleep during the day.*
How did you feel?	*I felt anxious* (primary emotion).
How did you react to the anxiety?	*I didn't like feeling anxious, and I wanted not to feel like that. My anxiety made it harder for me to explain what I was trying to say.*
What do you say to yourself?	*"I am mucking this up."* *"I should be able to make it clear what my needs are."* *"I am hopeless. I should be able to say what is on my mind."*
What did you feel then?	*I felt self-critical* (secondary emotion).
How did you react to the self-criticism?	*I didn't like the feeling. The feeling of self-criticism wasn't helping at all.*
What did you say to yourself?	*"I am so stupid. Why can't I just say what is on my mind."* *"If I can't explain myself, then my neighbour will not understand how important this is to me."* *"Get a grip and stop being so ridiculous."*
What did you feel then?	*I felt angry with myself* (secondary emotion).
How did you react to this feeling?	*I felt uncomfortable and stressed.*

What did you say to yourself?	*"I shouldn't feel angry because there is nothing to feel angry about."*
	"I am the one who is criticising myself, so there is no justification for feeling angry."
What did you feel then?	*I felt sad* (secondary emotion).

So, instead of just feeling anxious, you now feel anxious, self-critical, angry and sad. Your primary emotion is anxiety, and all the rest are secondary emotions.

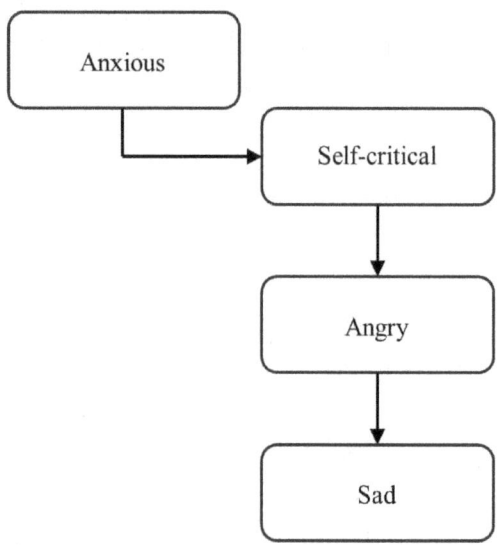

Figure 1: Diagram of primary emotion leading to secondary emotions.

One way to stop this process is to focus your attention and coping efforts on your presenting emotional state. For example, if you feel anxious then give this emotion your attention and work on ways to cope with your anxiety. The anxiety you are feeling is your primary emotion at that time. It is the emotion you feel directly because of what you are facing.

Your emotional reactions can be difficult to manage because what started as a straightforward emotional response to a stressful event turns into a confusing array of emotions. Sometimes, these emotions can compete with each other and pull you in different directions. For example, you can feel both sad and angry or angry and excited. Trying to deal with one of these emotions can be undermined by your efforts to deal with the other emotion.

Recognising and dealing with your emotions

There is a need to simplify things when you are dealing with difficult situations. You can learn to focus on your primary emotions as they arise and adopt strategies to deal with them. Let's start by looking at a way to identify your emotions so you know to what you should be giving your attention.

What happened?

> Here, consider the situation that developed that resulted in you feeling these strong emotions.

Why did this situation occur?

> Consider the possible causes of the problem situation. This is an important step. It gives you the opportunity to interpret the meaning of the problem situation in an effort to help you understand why you are feeling the strong emotions you are experiencing.

How were you feeling as a result of that situation?

> Try to identify your primary emotional response to the situation and then consider the secondary emotions you experience as well.

What is it that you wanted to do *as a result of how you were feeling?*

> Here, we refer to the urges or impulses you have to act in response to the emotional state you are in. When feeling strong emotions, people tend to experience urges to do more extreme actions.

> It does not follow that the person will always do these things, however, thoughts about doing them can be present. It is worth noting that people tend to *think* about doing extreme things much more often than they ever *do* them. What this means is that you control the impulse to act in a 'over the top' way. If you can control these impulses, you can control others in a way that will allow you to have a more settled and reasonable response to provoking situations.

What did you actually do and say?

> Here, you are considering what you actually did rather than what you had an urge to do.

After experiencing those emotions and actions, how did they affect you?

> Here, we are referring to the consequences for you of experiencing those strong emotional states and your reactions to those states by choosing to act in a particular way.

Let's start by taking the process of experiencing an emotional reaction a step at a time. Let's consider the example of you having to talk to your neighbour about the loud music.

Understanding your emotions worksheet - example
Time and date: *Thursday, 10th.*
What happened? *I had to have a discussion with my neighbour about how loudly they were playing music during the day when I am on night shift and trying to sleep. I became anxious because I didn't know how they were going to respond. I didn't want an argument. So, I ended up stumbling through the conversation and not doing a very good job at explaining myself.*
Why did this situation occur? *There are a couple of reasons I was in this situation. Firstly, I had to have this conversation with my neighbour because the music would have been too loud even if I didn't have to sleep. Even with my windows and doors closed, I could hear the bass noise thumping inside my house. Secondly, my anxiety affected me and influenced how I described the problem because my neighbour doesn't seem to be a person who would be very understanding of other people's difficulties. We have had some minor disagreements before.*
How were you feeling as a result of that situation? *I felt really anxious about speaking to my neighbour* (primary emotion) *and having to explain why I needed them to turn the volume down. Then, when I messed it up and didn't explain myself very well, I felt really stupid and self-critical* (secondary emotion) *because I should have been able to make it clear what I was experiencing. I then felt really angry* (secondary emotion), *not only because I had messed it up but because I then made myself feel worse than I would have otherwise if I had just been able to explain myself well. The fact that I was angry with myself then just made me feel sad* (secondary emotion).
What is it that you wanted to do as a result of how you were feeling? *I wanted to burst into tears and run away.*

What did you actually do and say?
I just kept trying to explain myself. I told myself there was nothing to feel anxious about. I figured the neighbour couldn't know I had a problem unless I told them. I should give them the opportunity to do the right thing. I then took a deep breath and tried to let go of some of the anxiety. I then tried a second time to explain myself, offering to let them know when I was on night shift so they could avoid playing music on those occasions.
After experiencing those emotions and actions, how did they affect you?
In the beginning, I felt like the problem was so big that it would never be solved. But, after I dealt with my anxiety by reminding myself I had nothing to keep feeling anxious about, and after taking a deep breath, I felt more able to explain my problem and offer a compromise.

To try and make sense of what you are feeling and why you are feeling it, we suggest you use the worksheet below. It is designed to help you to understand how you are reacting to the problems you are facing and this may direct you to how you can cope with the situation.

Understanding your emotions worksheet
Time and date:
What happened?
Why did this situation occur?

How were you feeling as a result of that situation?

What is it that you wanted to do as a result of how you were feeling?

What did you actually do and say?

After experiencing those emotions and actions, how did they affect you?

Worksheet available at elemen.com.au

Remember, here, your goal is to focus your attention on your primary emotion. If you can resolve your primary reaction to the problem you are facing, then other secondary emotions may either not occur or simply resolve. When you experience secondary emotions, tell yourself that you are going to focus your energy on your primary emotional reaction. You can then give your attention to finding ways to cope with the triggering source of your distress.

Does the size of your emotion fit your problem?

There is something else you can do to help regulate your emotions. In addition to the complexity of primary and secondary emotions, there is another factor that you should consider. Sometimes, we experience a strong emotion that is inconsistent with the size of the problem. That is, we might feel furious in response to a minor provocation when slightly annoyed would probably do the job. Let's examine this idea by first considering the range of emotions you might experience.

When you think about the range of emotions human beings experience, it can seem like an overwhelming number of feelings that would form an endless list if you decided to write them all down. To make sense of people's experience of emotions, there have been lots of complex conceptualisations of the types of emotions we experience.

Although it is interesting reading to learn of theorists' different views about our emotions, we are going to simplify the matter for the purpose of learning to regulate your emotional states. It is worth considering that, although we do have lots of emotional states, they tend to fall into four categories. The categories are as follows:

Glad

Mad

Sad

Bad

It is pretty much the case that any emotion you can think of would fall into one of these four categories. Let's take a moment to consider this. Below are some examples of the types of emotions that would fall into each category.

Table 2: Examples of emotions in each emotion state.

Emotion category	Examples of emotions
Glad	Happy, excited, joyful, content.
Mad	Annoyed, angry, furious, hostile.
Sad	Despondent, unhappy, miserable, forlorn.
Bad	Ashamed, disgusted, horrified, frightened.

When we examine the range of emotions we are capable of experiencing, it is apparent that some of these emotional states within each category are milder, and some are more intense or severe. An example might be the difference between content and ecstatic. Content is at the milder end of the 'glad' category, whereas ecstatic is at the extreme end.

When trying to make sense of your emotions, a good place to start is to put the emotions you are feeling into the appropriate category and to also consider the intensity of the emotion you are feeling. For example, in the sad category, you might be feeling mildly unhappy or you might be feeling quite miserable. In the mad category, there is clearly a difference between feeling annoyed and feeling furious.

There is one other thing you need to consider. We can develop a habit of experiencing severe or intense emotions when a milder emotion would be sufficient for the demands of the situation. Consider this example.

> *Laura had a habit of having angry meltdowns no matter what the severity of the provocation. Her parents said she had been like this since she was a child. They said her emotions would go from zero to one hundred at the drop of a hat. Laura had been having some problems with a neighbour. For the most part, the neighbour would do the wrong thing, and Laura would react. But, sometimes, she would overreact. For example, Laura's neighbour had left their rubbish bin on the footpath for a day after the garbage collection. Laura had spoken with them in the past about other problems, but they had never left their bin out overnight before. The wind was particularly strong that day, and the bin had been blown into her front yard. Although it did not damage anything, Laura had to go and take the bin and return it next door. She was furious. When her neighbour returned home, she berated them for failing to be responsible.*

Laura and others in her situation have a problem. Their emotions only have one speed – flat out. So, what happens when the triggering problem is only a minor one? It does not make any sense to have an intense emotional response in reaction to a minor problem.

In general, people like to have consistency between their emotional state and their perception of their problem. When you have a strong emotional response in reaction to a minor problem you can experience what is known as cognitive dissonance. This can occur when a person holds two opposing beliefs, that is, *I am feeling something very strongly* and *This is a minor problem.*

Cognitive dissonance is an uncomfortable experience. The person experiencing it will try to resolve this cognitive dissonance by bringing the two opposing beliefs into line with each other. In general, this would make the person feel more comfortable. So, rather than choose a different intensity of emotion, the person will simply view the problem as bigger than it deserves to be.

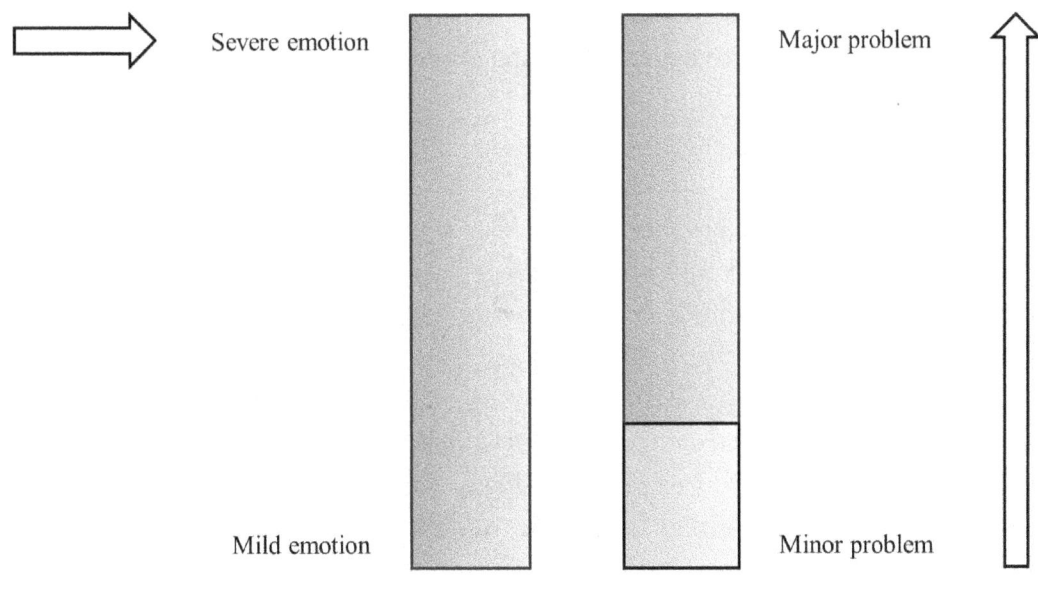

Figure 2: How cognitive dissonance causes an inflation in the perceived problem size.

From this diagram, you can see that if a person experiences the strongest emotion, they can push up the perceived severity of the problem they are experiencing to match the severity of the emotion. In our diagram, it is only the bottom portion of our problem column that represents the actual severity of the problem. However, because the person is experiencing a severe or intense emotional response, they identify the problem as much worse than it needs to be so that their emotion and the problem match. Although you would think that experiencing the emotion and the problem at the most extreme end of the scale would make a person feel worse, interestingly, it makes them feel better because there is then no disconnect between the emotion and the problem.

Let's revisit Laura.

> *Laura's neighbour had left their bin out overnight, and it had blown into Laura's front yard. Laura was furious. As she became increasingly worked up, she told herself that this was just another example of them being a terrible neighbour. There was no excuse for them leaving the bin out overnight. It was irresponsible. She suspected that they did it deliberately because she had complained about other things they had done, and this was their revenge. She decided she was not going to let them get away with it. They were going to learn never to do this sort of thing again.*

Laura turned a bin blown into her yard without it causing any damage into a major stressful life event. She did this because her strong emotional reaction was inconsistent with the minor problem, so she made the problem seem bigger. She then felt justified in feeling furious and any cognitive dissonance she might have felt did not emerge.

How might Laura have reacted differently?

> *Laura's neighbour had failed to take in their bin the night before, and it had blown into her yard. Laura had to go to the trouble of moving the bin back onto her neighbour's property. Despite the fact that she had had some difficulties with her neighbour in the past, Laura told herself that they had not left their bin out before. She was aware that it was very windy last night, so it was not surprising that the bin had blown onto her property. Laura thought she would just take the empty bin back to the neighbour's driveway. She was mildly annoyed about having to do that but she just started thinking about the other things she wanted to get done today.*

Rather than assigning the severity of the problem based on the intensity of the emotion you feel, it is better to determine the severity of the problem and then decide how much emotional energy you are going to give it. As you start to feel a strong emotion, ask yourself what is triggering it and how you are going to choose to feel in response to it.

For example, rather than being infuriated about some of the things the neighbours do to annoy you, it might be better to choose to feel mildly irritated. That feels like the right amount of emotion for a situation that is not overly disruptive to your life. Save 'infuriated' for an event that actually warrants that type of reaction. Notice that irritated and infuriated fall into the same emotion category (bad) but are on opposite ends of a scale from minor to severe.

We can look at a way to evaluate your problem size and its associated emotional state. Remember, you can examine your reactions in retrospect until you have better control of this tendency to make small problems bigger than they need to be. Use the following worksheet to examine how you reacted to an event and how you might have viewed things differently. Consider the following example.

	# Problem size worksheet - Example
What happened? *I realised I needed to talk to my neighbour about the music playing loudly when I needed to sleep when I was on night shift.*	
How did you feel about this at the time? *I felt so anxious, I couldn't settle. I was dreading having a conversation with the neighbour. I felt sick at the thought of having the discussion.*	
Rate the intensity of this feeling Mild| 1 2 3 4 5 6 7 **8** 9 10 |Severe	
What were you telling yourself? *I was thinking that I didn't know how my neighbour would respond. I thought they might become aggressive and shout at me.*	
Rate the perceived severity of the problem Minor| 1 2 3 4 5 6 7 **8** 9 10 |Serious	
How could you have looked at this problem differently? *I could have remembered that, although we had had some disagreements in the past, we had always been able to resolve them. I also could have remembered that at those time, my neighbour had never behaved aggressively towards me.*	
Rate the severity of this problem from this new perspective. Minor| **1** 2 3 4 5 6 7 8 9 10 |Serious	
What intensity of emotion should you give to this problem now? Mild| **1** 2 3 4 5 6 7 8 9 10 |Severe	

Below is a copy of the worksheet you can use to examine how you should react to problems that arise.

Problem size worksheet
What happened?
How did you feel about this at the time?
Rate the intensity of this feeling   Mild| 1   2   3   4   5   6   7   8   9   10 |Severe
What were you telling yourself?
Rate the perceived severity of the problem   Minor| 1   2   3   4   5   6   7   8   9   10 |Serious
How could you have looked at this problem differently?
Rate the severity of this problem from this new perspective.   Minor| 1   2   3   4   5   6   7   8   9   10 |Serious
What intensity of emotion should you give to this problem now?   Mild| 1   2   3   4   5   6   7   8   9   10 |Severe

Worksheet available at elemen.com.au

The importance of understanding this relationship between emotion and problem size is because there is a strong link between our emotional state and how we choose to behave. Strong, negative emotional states can drive us to behave in ways that we might not behave if we were not feeling so out of control emotionally. By learning to control our emotions, it makes it easier to behave in ways that benefit us rather than make the situation worse.

The link between emotions and behaviour

When you are dealing with difficult neighbours, you can feel strong emotions. This can be a difficult and uncomfortable time. It would be helpful for you to be able to manage those strong emotions.

This does not mean that you should fight against the emotions you feel. You cannot start a war with your emotional state and expect to be the victor. However, you cannot ignore your emotions and expect them to just disappear. The aim should be to recognise and validate your emotional reactions, but do what you can to avoid your emotional distress escalating.

It is worthwhile to understand the link between your emotional state and the things you choose to do in response to that emotion. This is important. It is difficult to control your behaviour choices if you do not appreciate the link between how you feel and what you do.

Let's consider how you might behave in relation to your emotional responses. Consider this example.

Imagine that you experienced an argument with the person who lives in the unit next door to yours. The small yards at the back of the units are separated by a fence but are quite close together. You had asked them not to smoke cigarettes near your shared fence as the smoke drifted over and entered your bathroom through the vented window. They were reluctant to agree and argued that they could do what they liked in their own backyard. They called you a busybody and told you to mind your own business.	
I felt	What I did
Angry	*I became increasingly infuriated with them and told them their attitude was terrible. I raised my voice and shouted. I called them selfish and said they were a horrible person. I stormed into my unit and slammed the door.*

The reaction in this example is not a helpful one. The person's emotional state drove them to increase the conflict then storm off.

Understanding this link between your emotional state and your behaviour can help you learn to make different choices in how you act when you are upset. Let's consider here how you might opt to do things differently. Consider the same example but now let's look at how this person might have chosen to behave in an alternative way.

I felt…	What I did	What I could have done instead
Angry	*I became increasingly infuriated with them and told them their attitude was terrible. I raised my voice and shouted. I called them selfish and said they were a horrible person. I stormed into my unit and slammed the door.*	*I could have remained calm and pointed out that getting upset did not resolve the problem. I could have invited my neighbour to work with me to come up with a solution to the problem of the smoke in my bathroom.*

Let's take this one step further and consider the likely outcomes of the initial behaviour choice and the alternative one.

I felt	*Angry*
I did…	*I became increasingly infuriated with them and told them their attitude was terrible. I raised my voice and shouted. I called them selfish and said they were a horrible person. I stormed into my unit and slammed the door.*
What happened?	*I continued to feel angry and upset. I stomped around my house and couldn't settle. The problem still existed, and I couldn't think of a way to resolve it.*
A better choice…	*I could have remained calm and pointed out that getting upset did not resolve the problem. I could have invited my neighbour to work with me to come up with a solution to the problem of the smoke in my bathroom.*
Likely outcome…	*I might have been irritated that my neighbour didn't immediately agree to stop smoking near the fence but, if I stayed calm, I could have gone on and made some suggestions about how to solve the problem, such as my neighbour smoking around the corner of his unit near his garage. I could have invited my neighbour to offer another solution if he could think of one.*

Initially, you can work on thinking up alternative and healthier behaviours after the event. This will allow you to learn how to make better choices by considering the different outcomes of various behaviours. It will then become easier to apply this strategy at the time you are feeling the emotional reaction so that you can choose the better behaviour at the time and avoid doing things that might feel all right in the moment but do not help you in the longer term. Below is a worksheet you can use.

The emotion-behaviour link worksheet
I feel/felt…
I did/I felt the urge to do…
What happened/what would have happened?
A better choice…
Likely outcome…

Worksheet available at elemen.com.au

You will feel better if your emotional state is more under your control. This does not protect you from strong emotions, but it allows you to handle them in manageable ways. Next, we can look at ways to manage how our nervous system reacts to stressful events.

Managing your stress and anxiety

It is important to understand your anxiety reactions as they are often experienced when you are confronted with disturbing behaviour from another person. You may know that you feel anxious, but you may not yet understand what is happening to you when you are feeling anxious. This can make your anxiety reactions even more unsettling than they need to be. So, let's consider how your nervous system works.

What is my nervous system doing?

Your autonomic nervous system (ANS) is the part of your nervous system that drives your functioning. It regulates your heart rate and temperature and makes other adjustments that are required for you to function on a moment-by-moment basis.

Your ANS is divided into two parts: the parasympathetic nervous system and the sympathetic nervous system. Your parasympathetic nervous system is the part of your ANS that should be driving you most of the time. It makes sure everything is ticking along so that your body gets what it needs and you can function well.

Your sympathetic nervous system has a specialised function. It is your self-protection system that automatically activates when you are under threat. So, if you were crossing the road and a truck came screaming around the corner, your sympathetic nervous system would activate so that you could quickly and efficiently move out of the way of the truck and reach safety. Adrenaline would release into your system, causing your hands to shake and your heart rate to increase, but you would reach the safety of the footpath on the other side of the road, and you would be fine. Your brain would then recognise that you were safe, and your sympathetic nervous system would turn off, and your parasympathetic nervous system would take over again.

Your sympathetic nervous system is attuned to your brain perceiving signs of threat. It activates when you are at risk of harm and prepares you to deal with that threat. It is an effective self-protection system when you are under threat. Unfortunately, for people who develop an overly sensitive sympathetic nervous system or for people who are dealing with ongoing conflict, their sympathetic nervous system will activate at the slightest indication that something is wrong and will prepare them to deal with the threat. This can occur even when there really is no threat to manage. This is what happens when you are anxious in the absence of an obvious cause of your anxiety, and this is the case when you are dealing with an ongoing conflict. In effect, your brain cannot distinguish between an external threat (e.g., a truck coming around the corner) and an internal threat (e.g., you thinking worrying or anxiety-provoking thoughts). An overly sensitive nervous system will rely on its self-defence mechanism to protect you from perceived harm.

Your nervous system will also react to crises in your life that do not present the same level of physical harm. Although it is stressful to be worrying all the time, this itself is not physically threatening to you. Nevertheless, your sympathetic nervous system can be triggered by your worrying thoughts. As stated, your brain cannot always make a distinction between an external threat to your physical integrity, and a threat to your emotional wellbeing that is caused by the way you are thinking.

Below is a table providing an overview of the activities of the parasympathetic and sympathetic nervous systems.

Table 3: The functions of the parasympathetic and sympathetic nervous systems.

	Parasympathetic	Sympathetic
Eyes	Constricts pupils	Dilates pupils
Salivary glands	Stimulates salivation	Inhibits salivation
Heart	Slows heartbeat	Accelerates heartbeat
Lungs	Constricts bronchi	Dilates bronchi
Stomach	Stimulates digestion	Inhibits digestion
Liver	Stimulates bile release	Simulates glucose release
Kidneys		Stimulates release of adrenaline and noradrenaline*
Intestines	Stimulates peristalsis and secretion	Inhibits peristalsis and secretion
Bladder	Contracts bladder	Relaxes bladder

* Also known as epinephrine and norepinephrine

When your sympathetic nervous system is activated, a series of physical changes occur that make sense if they are in response to a threat to your physical integrity. Some of these changes are listed below.

> Adrenaline is released so that you are alert and in a heightened state, ready to deal with the threat. This causes your heart rate to increase and can cause your hands, or even your whole body, to shake.

> Your hearing and your eyesight become better than normal. Everything sounds louder than it really is, and it is difficult to tolerate lots of light and movement. This is why anxious people tend to avoid places like supermarkets. Too much

noise, too much light, and too much movement can be overwhelming when you are feeling anxious. Anxious people tend to tolerate these things poorly because of the acuteness of their senses when their sympathetic nervous systems are activated. It helps to have really good hearing and eyesight if you are being threatened, but it does not help if you are just trying to do some shopping.

In our view, the most amazing thing that happens is that your sympathetic nervous system shuts down the systems it does not need to be using. For example, when under threat, your body needs to produce lots of glucose for energy, so it stimulates glucose production. However, other systems that are not needed are shut down. In particular, your sympathetic nervous system shuts down your gastrointestinal system (e.g., inhibits digestion and inhibits peristalsis and secretion, with peristalsis referring to the contraction of the muscles that push forward the contents of your digestive tract). This is all right if it is shut down for the period of time it takes for you to deal with a truck coming around the corner. Your body copes less well with your gastrointestinal system not functioning if the sympathetic nervous system activation is prolonged. You can lose your appetite, experience nausea, develop diarrhoea or, less commonly, constipation, and you can experience difficulty eating, or you will overeat to try to control the uncomfortable state of your digestive system.

All of these symptoms make sense if you are under threat but become a problem if the activation of your sympathetic nervous system is prolonged. Also, when your sympathetic nervous system is activated for reasons other than obvious threat, you can develop a sense of imminent danger just because your sympathetic nervous system has taken over your functioning. When your sympathetic nervous system is activated, your brain will interpret this as a sign that something is wrong. This explains why you feel this overwhelming sense that something terrible is going to happen and increases your worry.

Later, we will introduce some straightforward ways you can bring your sympathetic nervous system under better control so your anxiety and fear are reduced. You can learn to control what your nervous system does so that it does not overreact to difficult interactions with a neighbour.

Range of arousal

To understand how things work, you should be aware that human beings have a range of nervous system arousal within which we function the best. This range is quite large, from low in the range when we are very relaxed to high in the range when our nervous system is more 'revved up'. Pictured below is a diagram of this arousal range. The range within which you function best is known as the *window of tolerance*.

Within this window of tolerance, you have the flexibility to respond to the demands being placed on you. In this way, your arousal level will increase when you are faced with a demand and then decrease when that demand is over. As long as your arousal stays within this window, you will respond well to pressures placed on you.

If your arousal level drops below the lowest point of that range, you will enter a state of hypoarousal. In this state, you will feel slowed down and lethargic. Your functioning at this point will be inadequate, and your ability to respond to demands will be poor. If your arousal increases beyond the ceiling level, you will enter a state of hyperarousal. When this occurs, you can feel too aroused and can feel anxious and panicky. Your functioning will be impacted, and your ability to cope with pressures will deteriorate.

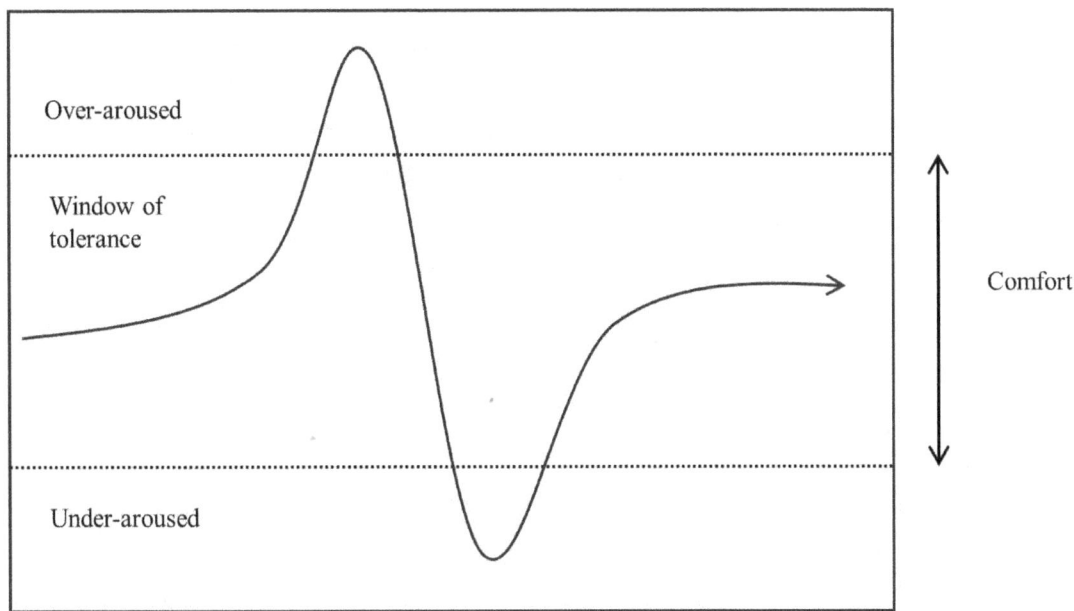

Figure 3: A diagram of the window of tolerance.

When you are dealing with a difficult neighbour, and these problems are ongoing, your arousal level creeps up from an optimal level of arousal in the middle of the window of tolerance to the upper extremes. You will find that you cannot or do not reduce that high level of arousal, even when you should be able to let go. This is why people cannot sleep well when they are under pressure. They can never relax enough for their arousal to decrease to a comfortable state. So, your 'baseline' arousal level, which is the starting point from which you respond to life demands, is high up in the range instead of midway.

So, your arousal level remains elevated. You barely notice this because it starts to feel normal to be under that much stress with your arousal level that high. But a problem exists. When any other thing occurs to which you have to respond, and the level of demand on you increases, your arousal level will increase to deal with that additional challenge. However, the starting point of your arousal level, or your baseline arousal level, is already so high that you have no room to move. Any increase in arousal will push you through the ceiling and into an uncomfortable and unpleasant hyperaroused state. You will experience intense anxiety as a result.

Your high starting point gives you no flexibility to respond or react to even minor additional stressors or an increase in worry or confusion about what to do with your life. So, the ways you normally cope with demanding situations fail because you have moved out of the range where you can successfully apply your usual coping strategies.

Your goal should be to get your nervous system back under control. Having faced ongoing difficulties with a neighbour, your arousal level may have been pushed to the upper limits of your window of tolerance. Any extra demands, even minor ones, cause your arousal level to move beyond the ceiling of the window of tolerance and uncomfortable and unpleasant anxiety symptoms are then experienced.

You need to aim to bring your optimal arousal level down to at least the middle of the window of tolerance, with a baseline or starting point, when you are at your most relaxed, to the lower end of that range. Remembering that it now feels almost normal to have your nervous system so 'revved up', you need to retrain your nervous system to have a better starting point and a better optimal arousal level.

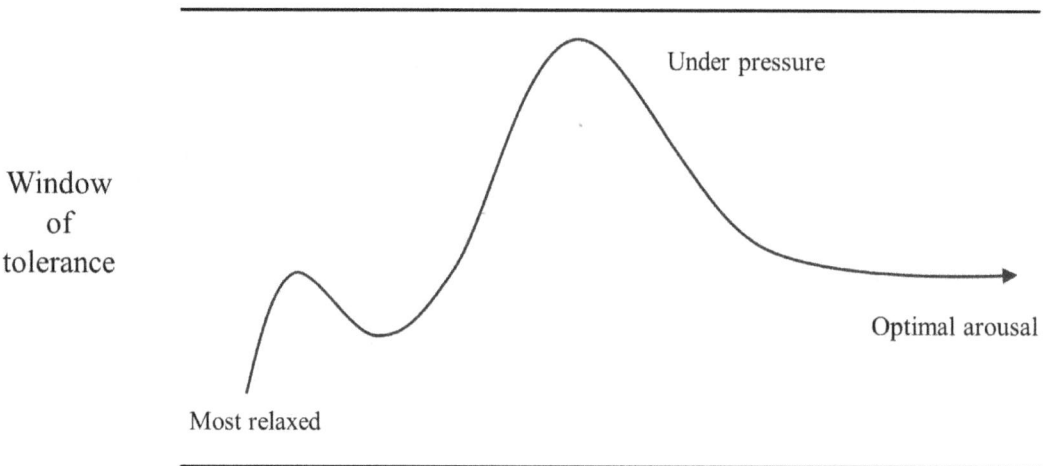

Figure 4: A diagram of an optimal arousal level.

We will introduce you to ways to control your anxiety. There are a variety of techniques you can use. You can try them all, but then you can choose the ones that best suit you and give you the greatest degree of nervous system control.

How to combat anxiety

How do you achieve anxiety management? Consider the following. When you are in an elevated or heightened state, at the top of your window of tolerance or beyond it, your heart rate increases and your breathing changes. Your heart rate elevation is caused by a release of adrenaline that occurs when your sympathetic nervous system is triggered. This can be very uncomfortable, and it feels like there is very little you can do about it.

Your breathing changes contribute to the elevation in your heart rate. When people are stressed, their breathing tends to be rapid and shallow. You can liken this pattern of breathing to the waves on top of the water. Form a picture in your mind of the way a child draws waves. When we are stressed, we tend to breathe in sharply, then breathe out quickly and then breathe in again quickly. You tend not to breathe all the way out before you breathe in again. This inhalation-exhalation pattern is what affects your heart rate.

In contrast, when you are relaxed, your breathing tends to be deeper and slower and has a pattern that is similar to the swell in the ocean. The inhalation-exhalation pattern is a comfortable breath-in followed by a long, slower breath-out. You do not breathe in again until you have breathed all the way out.

From the diagram below, you can see the pattern of anxious, rapid and shallow breathing on the top. Below that is the pattern of slower, deeper breathing that is characteristic of a more relaxed state.

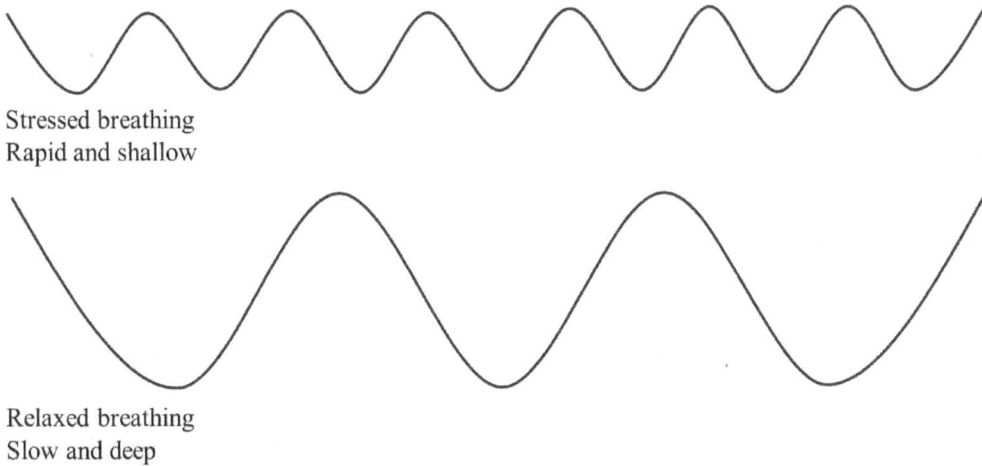

Figure 5: A comparison of stressed and relaxed breathing.

The reason your breathing pattern affects your heart rate is because these two things are linked. Under normal, stress-free conditions, your heart rate increases as you breathe in and then slows as you breathe out. This is normal.

When you are stressed your respiration rate increases and your breathing is shallower, your heart rate does not have a chance to slow before you breathe in again. Therefore, your heart rate is elevated and stays up.

Let's, for a moment, go back to the truck speeding around the corner, threatening to run you over. Your sympathetic nervous system is activated, allowing you to be in the right physical state to move quickly out of harm's way and protect yourself. When you get to the other side of the road, the truck goes past, and you are unharmed; your brain registers these experiences, your sympathetic nervous system turns off, and your parasympathetic nervous system takes over. This is because reaching the other side of the road and seeing the truck pass you by are safety signals. Your brain interprets these signs as indicators that you are going to be all right.

Of course, no such safety signals are available when you are going over the difficulties you are having with a neighbour in your mind. This is not the sort of thing that allows for a safety signal. Your brain would struggle to identify safety indicators because they do not exist in that sort of form. What you can do is offer your brain a safety signal but of a different type.

You can send a message that everything is all right by deliberately slowing your heart rate from its elevated rate to a more normal rate for you. Although it sounds difficult to achieve, controlling your heart rate is actually a reasonably straightforward undertaking. If you slow your breathing and lengthen your exhalation until you have breathed all the way out before breathing back in, your heart rate will come into line with your respiration rate, and your heart rate will go down.

To use our waves and ocean swell analogy, the aim is to change the pattern of your breathing from waves on the top of the water to a pattern like the swell in the ocean, where the water is lifted up and then put back down as the swell passes. You are aiming for an easy, comfortable breath in, followed by a long, slow breath out.

The ideal situation is to breathe out for twice as long as it takes you to breathe in. Lengthening your breath out requires that you slow the amount of air you breathe out so that you can breathe out for longer. You should aim to breathe all the way out, emptying your lungs, before you gently and comfortably breathe back in.

This pattern of breathing should result in a slowed heart rate and a subsequent reduction in that sense of anxiety or crisis that occurs when your sympathetic nervous system is triggered. This occurs because your brain interprets the reduction in heart rate and the change in breathing pattern as a signal that the crisis is over.

Let's consider a simple exercise to control your breathing by deepening your breaths and slowing them down.

	Slowing and controlling your breathing
1.	Without trying to change your breathing, just notice for a moment the pattern of your inhalations and exhalations.
2.	Now, take a comfortable breath in. It does not have to be too deep, rather just a comfortable breath.
3.	Now, breathe out, slowing the amount of air you exhale and lengthening your breath as a result.
4.	When your lungs feel empty of air, gently and comfortably breathe back in.
5.	As you breathe, practice lengthening your exhalation just a bit. You may also deepen your breath in slightly. Keep in mind the picture of the ocean swell if this helps.
6.	Practice this pattern of breathing for as long as you feel comfortable.

Exercise available at elemen.com.au

There is another element that you can add to this breathing exercise that may help with your ultimate goal of reducing your anxiety and signalling your sympathetic nervous system to turn off so your parasympathetic nervous system can do its job. You can include in this breathing exercise the element of reducing your muscle tension.

People who are stressed tend to have tense muscles. Although this muscle tension can occur anywhere in the body, common sites include the forehead and scalp, neck, jaw, shoulders, and chest. The increased muscle tension contributes to the overall sense of readiness to deal with threat. On the downside, tense muscles can cause headaches, chest and other pain.

If tense muscles present a significant problem for you, then a progressive muscle relaxation exercise may help. A general overview of this technique is provided below. More comprehensive versions are available online. However, another easy strategy is to link the relaxation of muscles with the breathing exercise.

As you breathe out, just relax your muscles in places where they feel tight and tense. You do not have to achieve marked muscle relaxation to experience a noticeable difference. Just drop your shoulders, relax your jaw, smooth your forehead or relax your stomach muscles. Aim for a gentle relaxation of tight muscles as you exhale.

The combination of breathing exercises and muscle relaxation can be used even when the focus is on controlling your breathing. You can also use the combined technique when your primary focus is on troubling muscle tension. In combination, the techniques can help with either target.

	Combined breathing and muscle relaxation technique
1.	Take a comfortable breath in. It does not have to be too deep, but rather just a comfortable breath.
2.	Now, breathe out, slowing the amount of air you exhale and lengthening your breath as a result. As you breathe out, drop your shoulders, relax your jaw, smooth your forehead and relax your abdominal muscles.
3.	When your lungs feel empty of air, gently and comfortably breathe back in.
4.	As you breathe, practice lengthening your exhalation just a bit. You may also deepen your breath in slightly. Keep in mind the picture of the ocean swell if this helps. Continue to relax your muscles slightly on each exhalation.
5.	Practice this pattern of breathing and muscle relaxation for as long as you feel comfortable.

Exercise available at elemen.com.au

As stated, if muscle tension presents you with a significant problem, you may wish to try a method of progressive muscle relaxation. This technique involves tensing your muscles and then relaxing them. Tensing your muscles before relaxing them has a number of purposes. It helps you to clearly identify where the tension in your body is located. It helps you feel the difference between a tense muscle and a relaxed one, which is helpful when the muscle has been tense for a long time. Finally, tensing the muscle first helps to induce deeper relaxation in that muscle when you relax it.

We will start with a longer version of the progressive muscle relaxation exercise that will help you learn the technique. You can then change to a shorter version that we describe below.

	Progressive muscle relaxation (longer version)
1.	Choose a comfortable place where it is quiet. Lay down or sit in a comfortable position with your feet flat on the floor.
2.	Now, clench both your fists… tighter and tighter. Notice the tension in your muscles. Keep them clenched for about 10 seconds. Now relax. Feel your muscles relax. Notice the difference between the tension and relaxation.
3.	Repeat the same procedure with your fists. Notice the difference between tension and relaxation.

4.	Now, bend your elbows on both arms and tense your biceps. Hold the tension. Now relax. Notice the difference between tension and relaxation.
5.	Repeat the same procedure with your elbows bent and your biceps tensed. Hold the tension, then relax. Pay attention to the change from tension to relaxation.
6.	Now, frown as hard as you can. Notice the tension in your forehead. Hold the tension. Now relax. Notice the difference you feel after you have released the tension.
7.	Now, frown again as hard as you can. Hold the tension, then release it. Notice the contrast between tension and relaxation.
8.	Now, close your eyes and squint them tightly. Hold the tension then relax. Allow your eyes to feel a comfortable relaxed state. Notice the change. Repeat by closing your eyes and squinting then relaxing, letting go of the tension.
9.	Now, clench your jaw. Bite down hard. Notice the tension throughout your jaw. Now, relax your jaw, allowing your teeth to fall apart slightly. Notice the feeling of relaxation. Repeat this exercise with your jaw.
10.	Now, press your tongue hard against the roof of your mouth. Hold it there. Feel the tension at the back of your mouth. Now relax. Notice the difference between the tension and relaxation. Repeat the exercise with your tongue.
11.	Now, purse your lips, pushing them out into an 'O' shape. Hold them there. Now release the tension and relax. Notice how your mouth feels now that it is relaxed. Repeat the exercise with your lips.
12.	Now, press your head back as far as it will comfortably go. Hold onto the tension. Roll your head from the right to the left, allowing the focus of the tension to change. Now relax. Feel the difference between the tension in your neck and the relaxation. Repeat the exercise by pressing your head back.
13.	Now, bring your head forward with your chin on your chest. Feel the tension in your throat and the back of your neck. Hold the tension, then relax and allow your head to return to a comfortable position. Repeat the exercise by bringing your head forward.

14.	Now, shrug your shoulders, bringing your shoulders up and allowing your head to hunch down between them. Hold the tension. Now relax and notice the difference between tension and relaxation.
15.	Now, breathe in deeply and hold your breathe. Hold it. Now allow yourself to gently exhale, letting go of tension as you breathe out. Feel your body relax. Repeat the exercise, breathing in then gently letting go.
16.	Now, tense your stomach muscles. Hold onto the tension. Now relax. Let your stomach muscles relax and appreciate that feeling. Repeat the exercise with your stomach muscles.
17.	Now, arch your back without straining. Hold onto the tension. Now, let it go. Notice the change in your muscles. Now repeat the exercise by arching your back.
18.	Now, tighten your buttocks and thighs. Press down on your heels to flex your thigh muscles. Hold onto the tension. Now relax and notice the difference. Repeat the exercise.
19.	Now, curl your toes downward to cause your calves to tense. Hold onto the tension. Now relax. Repeat the exercise.
20.	Now, draw your toes upward, causing your shins to feel tense. Pay attention to the tension. Now relax. Repeat the exercise.
21.	Now, scan your body. Notice if there are any tense spots. Repeat the exercise in that area.
22.	Enjoy a more relaxed feeling throughout your entire body. When you are ready, slowly return to your normal activities, holding on to that feeling of relaxation.

Exercise available at elemen.com.au

Once you have learned the technique, you can use a shorter version. You may prefer to just focus on the areas of your body that are particularly tense. It is certainly the case that some people tend to carry their muscle tension in one or two areas. Here is a shorter version that will allow you to tailor the procedure to suit your own needs.

	Relaxing using progressive muscle relaxation (short version)
1.	Choose a comfortable place where it is quiet. Lay down or sit in a comfortable position with your feet flat on the floor.
2.	Begin to work your way through groups of muscles by tensing them and relaxing them. For example, if you start with your forehead, tighten the muscles in your forehead by frowning. Hold for a few moments (10-15 seconds), then release, allowing the muscle in your forehead to relax, enjoying that experience for about 60 seconds. Notice the difference between the tension and the relaxation.
3.	Then, move on to the next group of muscles. You can work through groups of muscles from the top of your head to the tips of your toes, or you can select areas of your body that present a particular problem of tension for you.
4.	Repeat the process until you have worked your way through the groups of muscles you have selected.
5.	Repeat that process again, first tensing the muscles, holding that tension for five to ten seconds, and then relaxing those muscles.

Exercise available at elemen.com.au

So, controlling your breathing and, thus, lowering your heart rate will help you feel less anxious, as will reducing your muscle tension. However, there are other approaches you can take to anxiety management.

More exercises to help

One of the problems with being anxious and 'revved up' is that your mind fills up with anxiety-provoking thoughts. This is the basis of stress and worry. When you are focused on trying to make sense of what is happening to you, you cannot seem to stop thinking in an endless stream of anxiety-provoking thoughts. This makes it very difficult to get your nervous system back under control. The thoughts racing through your mind do not allow you to relax. So, included here are some exercises that should help you settle your mind.

The first exercise aims to teach you to self-soothe. If you can learn to settle yourself, the racing thoughts in your mind may follow. The quieter your nervous system, the less active your mind is with anxiety-provoking thoughts.

What you are aiming to do is find ways to soothe yourself. Most of us can understand how we go about soothing an upset child. We might hold and rock a distressed child and say soothing things. What you are looking for are adult versions of self-soothing strategies that will help to alleviate your distressed state.

The goal of developing self-soothing strategies is to create for yourself some moments of less distress. The strategies are aimed at reducing your heightened state to a more manageable level. They allow your nervous system's arousal level to be brought back under your control. So, strategies that allow you to focus on the here-and-now are the ones that will allow you to choose to be in a quieter state with a greater sense of peace of mind.

Consider the proposed self-soothing strategies listed below and select ones that you think might assist you. These may be things you have tried before or ones you feel might work for you. Some of these strategies require you to make the effort to seek out the means of engaging with them. However, others are using things that are readily available or easily obtained.

	Self-soothing strategies
1.	Take a shower or a warm bath. Focus your attention on the sensations created by the water. Enjoy the feeling of the water on your skin and the warmth of the water.
2.	Play with your pet, or just stroke your dog's or cat's coat. Interacting with your pet has been demonstrated to be soothing for many pet owners.
3.	Change into your most comfortable clothes. Enjoy the feel of the fabric and the degree of comfort you feel from wearing these items of clothing.
4.	Go for a swim. Enjoy the sensation of being in the water. Allow those sensations to quiet your mind. Even if you are not a good swimmer, bobbing around in the water can produce the same sensations.
5.	Treat yourself to a massage if that appeals to you. Allow your muscles to relax and your mind to quiet.
6.	Listen to soothing music. Allow your attention to be directed to the music rather than have the music in the background.
7.	Listen to an audiobook, even if your distress makes it difficult to concentrate. Try to pay attention to each word that is spoken. If you lose track of the story, you can always return to the previous track and pick up the story again.
8.	Turn on the television or talkback radio and engage in listening to what is being broadcast. The goal here is to focus your attention on the conversations as they play out rather than selecting a programme you are excited to watch or listen to. It is the process of listening to others talking that is soothing.

9.	Listen to the sounds of water running. Again, the aim is to listen to the sounds of the water, stopping your mind from going to other intrusive thoughts. You can find the sound of running water in various places. You can visit a naturally occurring water course or waterfall. You could listen to running water from an outdoor garden fountain. However, you can also get an indoor personal fountain that can be used at any time. Alternatively, you can listen to recorded sounds of water running.
10.	Find something soothing to look at. This might be by the water or an outdoor space such as a park. It could be photographs or paintings that you find soothing or relaxing. The goal is to find something to look at that is engaging for you, and that you find relaxing and soothing.

Exercise available at elemen.com.au

Managing anxiety-related thoughts

Before considering ways to change your thinking from being focused on the problems you are experiencing with a difficult neighbour, it is worth mentioning here some straightforward strategies for managing the sense of threat that anxious arousal causes. Although focusing on managing the physical manifestations of anxiety and focusing on quieting your nervous system can assist you, there is also value in quieting your anxious mind.

Simple threat reduction strategy

To start, there is a simple strategy that can help quiet a stressed mind that is repeatedly going over thoughts about what is happening to you. People who are facing this dilemma tend to cast their minds into the future, trying to decide what to do. Too little attention is paid to the present. The anxiety you feel about the future destroys any peace of mind you might be able to have in the present.

Threat reduction strategy	
The strategy involves the following easy steps:	
1.	Catch yourself thinking stressful thoughts.
2.	Evaluate your immediate environment for any signs of threat.
3.	Ask yourself if there is anything you need to do right now in relation to the thing you are focusing on in your thoughts.
4.	Give yourself permission to let go of your anxiety and concern for the time being.

Exercise available at elemen.com.au

Exercises in quieting your mind

There are strategies available for quieting your mind. Building on the notion of self-soothing, it is a good idea to be more present in your focus. If you give it some consideration, you will find that the thoughts racing through your mind when you are anxious typically are not related to what is happening in the here and now. Our thoughts tend to be time-travelling; that is, they are focused either on what has already happened or what is to come. They rarely focus on what is happening in the present moment when you are trying to relax and get your worry under control.

Usually, at these times, nothing is happening that is worth being concerned about. If you could deliberately spend more time focused on the here and now and less time on the past or future, you would have a better chance of relaxing and quieting your overly stimulated nervous system.

The notion of focusing on the here and now is based on mindfulness techniques. Mindfulness refers to your ability to be aware of your emotions, your physical state, your actions and your thoughts in a state of mind that is absent from judgment or criticism of your experience. Research has demonstrated that mindfulness helps you to control symptoms of anxiety, to control the distress caused by particular situations, to increase your capacity to relax, and to learn how to cope better with challenging situations.

Based on the notion of mindfulness, we have included some exercises you can use to quiet your mind by focusing on the here and now. To do this well, you may need to practice the skill. When you first learn these techniques, it is easy to become distracted and return to your racing thoughts. Do not worry if this happens. Just return to your exercise and continue.

Mindful listening	
1.	Sit in a comfortable place, preferably by yourself. If you wish, close your eyes.
2.	Start to focus your attention on the sounds around you.
3.	Notice the changes in the sounds from moment to moment.
4.	Notice the times between sounds when it is quiet.
5.	Focus your attention both on what is happening inside and outside.
6.	Pay attention to the sounds and nothing else. Do not make judgments about the sounds. Just acknowledge the sound then listen to the next one.
7.	If thoughts about other things come into your mind, put them aside and then return to listening to the sounds around you.
8.	Do this for a few minutes or until you are ready to stop.

Exercise available at elemen.com.au

Let's try another mindfulness exercise.

Mindful use of your senses	
Sight	Look around you. Allow your attention to be drawn to five things in your immediate environment that you might not normally pay any attention to. For example, this might be the way the fruit is sitting in the fruit bowl, the way your curtain is hanging, or the way your books are placed on your bookcase. Allow your attention to rest on each of these things. Keep your focus directed at the item, setting aside any other thoughts that come into your mind.
Touch	Bring your attention to four things you can feel at this moment in time. For example, it may be the feel of the sun on your skin, or the feel of the fabric of your clothes against your skin, or the feel of the chair underneath you, or the feel of the table surface where your hand is resting. Allow your attention to rest on each of these feelings. Keep your focus directed at each sense of touch, setting aside any other thoughts that come into your mind.

Hearing	Listen to the sounds in your surroundings. Notice three things you can hear. For example, you might hear the sounds of cars travelling along the road, the noise of the refrigerator, or the sound of the wind in the trees. Focus your attention on each of these sounds. If other thoughts come into your mind, let those thoughts go and return to focusing on the sounds you can hear.
Smell	Pay attention and search for two things you can smell. For example, you might be able to smell whatever you are cooking, the scent of plants in your garden, or the sea air if you live near the water. Keep your attention focused on each of these smells. If other distracting thoughts come into your mind, let these thoughts go and return to focusing on the things you can smell.
Taste	When you are eating, focus your attention on the tastes you are experiencing. For example, take a sip of your coffee and notice the taste. Bite into your sandwich and notice the flavours. Really pay attention to the flavours of the things you are tasting. If you become distracted, let go of these interfering thoughts and return to focusing on the things you are tasting.

Exercise available at elemen.com.au

And there is one last mindfulness exercise.

	Mindful walking
1.	As you are about to begin your walk, stand still for a moment. Sense the weight on your feet as you stand there. Feel how your muscles are supporting you and maintaining your stability and balance. Be aware of your arms in a comfortable position of your choice (e.g., by your side or hands clasped, either at the front or at your back). Allow yourself to stand there, relaxed but alert.
2.	Begin to walk. Choose a comfortable pace, not too fast and not too slow. Pay attention to how your feet and legs feel (e.g., their heaviness or lightness, the energy, or even any pain). The way your legs and feet feel will form the focus of your attention. If you become distracted, return to focusing on your legs and feet.
3.	Pay attention to the way in which you lift your feet and place them back down on the surface on which you are walking. Notice how you lift your foot, swing your leg and place your foot down again ahead of where you were a moment before. Walk in a natural and relaxed manner. Move your arms in a way that feels normal for you.

4.	It is likely that your mind will wander as you walk along. Your attention will be drawn to what is around you or thoughts that come into your mind. Acknowledge that you have been distracted and return to focusing on the process of walking… the lifting of your foot, the swing of your leg and the placement of your foot in front of you. Just gently return your attention to the sensations of walking.
5.	You might focus on a point ahead of you. Focus on the steps you take as you move towards that point. One step at a time. Experience fully the sensations of walking.
6.	Keep walking mindfully until you reach your destination or the point where you decide to turn around and mindfully walk back to where you started.

Exercise available at elemen.com.au

These types of strategies can help deal with the anxiety that is triggered by dealing with a difficult neighbour. However, anxiety is only one of a range of emotions you can experience when you are dealing with such a stressful situation. One emotional reaction that you might find difficult to control in such situations is anger.

Managing your anger

It should be noted that there are times when your increased nervous system arousal will manifest as an angry response rather than an anxious one, especially when you are dealing with difficult interactions with a neighbour. You might find yourself raising your voice or becoming overwhelmed by frustration and annoyance. You might act out in ways that you would not do if you were in a calmer state of mind. Certainly, at these times, you can act in a way that does not make you feel good about yourself when you reflect on what you have done.

If you have a more significant anger control problem, then we recommend that you seek a workbook that focuses on more extensive ways in which you can learn to control your anger or seek out professional help. However, here we would like to focus on some simple ideas that may help you control your angry feelings. Firstly, we will teach you a simple strategy to manage an angry response.

To understand why this strategy is effective, you need to consider that anger tends to be experienced in an escalating manner. That is an angry response is triggered and then gets worse when one or both of two things happen. The first is that you can think anger-provoking thoughts that will build your anger. These thoughts tend to relate to things not being the way you want them to be and your feeling that what you are experiencing is not justified and should not be happening.

The second refers to a process of reaction to how the other person responds to your anger that escalates the angry interaction. That is, an initial angry comment can be made, and the other person then becomes angry, so you become more angry, and then the other person's anger increases further. This escalating pattern leads to uncontrolled anger.

So, what should you do if you find your anger being triggered or it is escalating?

Exit and wait strategy

The most straightforward strategy you can use to stop the escalation of your anger and allow it to abate is an exit and wait strategy. When you are feeling angry, leave the situation and wait until you are calm before you return. It is an easy and effective strategy. Walk out of the room and allow yourself to calm down.

When away from the anger-provoking situation, there are a couple of tips you can use to help you calm down more quickly. Firstly, avoid going over the angry situation in your mind. This only aggravates your anger and makes it harder for you to settle down. So, when you leave the room, try to think about something else. Distract yourself by focusing on something that will hold your attention. Secondly, you can physically control your angry reaction by slowing your breathing and relaxing your tense muscles. This allows you to bring your nervous system over-arousal under control.

When you are calm and better able to handle the situation, return to what you were doing when the angry response was triggered. Go back with the right frame of mind. Decide that you are going to disengage from the interaction that caused the problem. Being calmer will give you a better chance of thinking clearly and articulating what you want to convey to your neighbour.

Another strategy is to adopt a spectator role by simply observing what you are doing without interpreting and judging. Observe how your neighbour is behaving without feeling you are fully engaged. This requires that you take a step back and watch how the interaction is playing out. In this way, you are choosing not to fully immerse yourself in a conflict situation. You can engage enough to know what is going on without feeling like what is happening is a direct threat to you. This will help you to continue with the interaction while reducing the risk of further escalations of anger.

Controlling thoughts that trigger anger

While the exit and wait technique is an emergency control strategy, you may need something more complex to effectively deal with your angry feelings. We can start by examining the types of thoughts that trigger angry feelings.

In a general sense, angry thoughts are triggered by a particular point of view that serves to justify our right to be angry. This point of view is made up of the following thought combination:

> I have been harmed or victimised by the other person.
>
> This person harmed me or victimised me deliberately.
>
> This person should not have done this; they were wrong; they should have chosen to act differently and in a way that would not harm or victimise me.

These thoughts tend to underlie most angry interactions. If you broke your angry thoughts into their particular elements, you would be able to discern the following:

> The harm done.
>
> The way it was done deliberately.
>
> Why this was wrong.

However, it should be remembered that this is your *perception* of the situation rather than the *facts* of the situation. How right or wrong you are in your perception is not determined by what you see as your justifiable anger. That is, your anger does not make these things true. Rightness or wrongness will be determined by the facts of the matter.

Unfortunately, it is hard to consider the facts when you are in an angry state. In effect, you are blinded by your emotional state and you are not in a position to think things through clearly.

Also, even if it is the case that someone has done the wrong thing, it does not mean that you cannot choose what way you will respond to this. It does not follow that you have to feel anger in response to someone else's actions. For example, you may choose to just shrug your shoulders about their behaviour and ignore their attempts to rile you.

Instead of just focusing on the situation that triggered your anger, you may be better served to think of ways that would allow you to control how you respond. This allows you to take responsibility for the outcome rather than being a helpless victim of someone else's poor behaviour. Consider the following example.

Changing my reaction – Example 1
What happened to provoke my anger? *I live by the motto, "Early to bed, early to rise…". The problem is that my neighbours like to spend their summer evenings swimming in their backyard pool and sitting on their deck chatting and enjoying each other's company. Their entertainment area is well-lit, and although they don't make a lot of noise, I can hear their chatter, and the light shines into my bedroom and disturbs me. My request that they not use their backyard in the evenings was ignored.*
How did I interpret this event? *I interpreted this as my neighbours being disrespectful and intrusive. I viewed their rejection of my request to be considerate of my preference to go to bed early as deliberately provocative on their part. I believe what they are doing is unfair.*
What did I think should happen? *I thought they should not use their backyard in the evenings because it makes it hard for me to sleep.*
How could I think differently about this situation? *I could see that, in fact, it is normal enough for people to want to enjoy summer nights outdoors. In truth, they weren't being overly loud, and it was more the light that was bothering me. They are not doing anything they are not permitted to do, even if I would prefer they didn't do it.*
How is this likely to make me feel? *If I changed the way I thought about this situation, it might open me up to thinking of other ways to solve the problem. As a result, I wouldn't feel so angry. In fact, if I could think of other ways to solve the problem (thicker curtains, asking them to use a lower-wattage light bulb), I probably wouldn't feel anything at all about them using their backyard when they wanted.*

Let's consider another example.

Changing my reaction – Example 2
What happened to provoke my anger? *Every year, the fruit on the trees overhanging my fence from the neighbour's yard drops in my garden, and I have to clean it up. Now, it is that time of year again, and I am again faced with having to clean up their mess. I told them the tree had to be removed, but they didn't want to consider doing that.*
How did I interpret this event? *They know this is a problem, but they never do anything about it. They pick the fruit they can reach but then deliberately leave the rest to fall into my garden. They are deliberately trying to upset me. They should have done something about it before now, and they could have done something to fix it if they had wanted to.*
What did I think should happen? *I thought they should cut down the tree and stop trying to cause me problems.*
How could I think differently about this situation? *I could maybe realise there might be other ways to solve this problem. Maybe they would be willing to do something, or the problem could be fixed if I hadn't been so hostile when I spoke with them. If I was acting in a less hostile manner, I could make an arrangement to use the fruit on my side of the fence (which I didn't want to do just to make a point that their tree was causing me problems), or I could invite them to come onto my property to collect the fruit from that side of the tree.*
How is this likely to make me feel? *I think I would be happier if we had a plan set in place to deal with the fruit falling from the tree.*

It is a good idea for you to work through your reactions to anger-provoking situations to see if you can re-interpret them in a way that helps you control your angry feelings. It is worth keeping in mind that angry feelings can be unpleasant and can drive you to do things that you might not choose to do if you were calmer. You can use the worksheet below to go through this process of reframing your response to anger-provoking situations.

Changing my reaction worksheet
What happened to provoke my anger?
How did I interpret this event?
What did I think should happen?
How could I think differently about this situation?
How is this likely to make me feel?

Worksheet available at elemen.com.au

If your angry reactions are just a reflection of the situation you are in, then these steps may help you manage those reactions and help you choose to react differently and in a way that is advantageous to you. This can help you settle your nervous system and feel more in control. Certainly, without reactive anger, you can begin to think differently and more clearly about your situation.

Managing your sleep disturbance

There are two ways that your sleep can be disturbed as a result of a neighbour's behaviour. The first is externally generated. That is, your sleep is directly interrupted by the behaviour of a neighbour. The most common way this occurs is when neighbours make excessive noise during the night when most people would be trying to sleep.

The second way your sleep can be disturbed is internally generated. That is, your sleep disturbance is a direct result of the stress you are feeling in the context of difficulties with a neighbour.

Externally generated sleep disturbance

A neighbour's behaviour can interfere with your ability to sleep when the nature of that behaviour is not conducive to sleep. The most obvious reason is that your neighbour is producing too much noise at a time when others are trying to sleep.

Some neighbours seem not to have a volume switch and everything they do seems to be loud. For these neighbours, going about their usual activities seems to create excessive noise. They slam their doors, they rattle their garbage bins, their voices are loud, the volume on their televisions is turned up too far, and they rev their car engines. Although not deliberately engaging in behaviours that would be considered to be problematic for people trying to sleep, they cause a problem because they seem to be louder than the average person, especially for the light sleeper.

Other neighbours engage in behaviours that would be problematic for most people when they are trying to sleep. These neighbours have parties with music blaring, they listen to high volume, bass-thumping music at night, they congregate in their yards late at night without regard to the noise they generate, they believe that the crack of dawn is a good time to mow their lawn, and they work on their motorbike into the night.

It is often the case that the neighbours in the latter group are breaching noise restrictions in their neighbourhood. Although it can feel reassuring to know that you have the law on your side, forcing people to abide by these restrictions can be hard to achieve. Although someone may come and tell your neighbour to quieten down if you make a complaint about a rowdy party, in general, it is likely that you would have to endure many sleepless nights before anything was done to enforce a noise regulation.

What can I do about my externally generated sleep problems?

When your sleep is being disturbed by externally generated noise from a neighbour, there is a variety of things you can do to manage the disturbance. Most obviously, you can inform your neighbour that the noise is causing you a problem and you can ask them to modify their behaviour. Whether you feel able to do this may be determined by the nature of your relationship with your neighbour. If a hostile relationship already exists, you may not feel comfortable making such a request.

Also, a factor that might impact your decision about whether to approach your neighbour with such a request is the character of your neighbour. It is unlikely you would feel comfortable having a chat with your neighbour about their level of noise if that person is perceived to be intimidating or threatening.

So, there are genuine reasons why you might not choose to approach your neighbour, point out the problem you are experiencing and request a change in their behaviour. If you do not feel able to have this discussion with your neighbour, you need to find an alternative strategy to manage the problem.

You may choose to use a means of blocking the noise. This may be ear plugs or noise cancelling headphones. There are sleep headphones available on the market that lay flat against your head and are held in place by a soft band around your head. These may be more comfortable than normal headphones and are more likely to stay in place as you sleep.

You may choose to override the noise. You can do this by having white noise playing. This is unlikely to disturb your sleep once you are used to it. If you prefer, there are sleep-assisting sound recordings available. Examples include the sound of rain, jungle noises, bird calls, waves on the sand, or whale calls. Choose one that you would find soothing.

If your irritation level is high because of the external noise, you can keep a notebook by your bedside and record your thoughts and feelings to get the irritation off your chest. Write down how long the noise has gone on for, what you are thinking, and how you are feeling. If it helps, you can use a bit of creative licence and use language that is humorous or colourful.

Remember, if the noisy behaviour of the neighbour is breaching noise regulations in your area, you have the right to call the police. If enough neighbours complain and complain often, the neighbours might learn that it is not appropriate to disturb the people around them with their inconsiderate behaviour.

Also, remember to stay calm and do not retaliate. It does not help to enter into a competition about who can be the most inconsiderate neighbour. Maintain the moral high ground and do what you can to protect yourself and your sleep.

Internally generated sleep disturbance

As stated, one of the consequences of your nervous system being revved up and you being stressed about difficult neighbours is that your sleep can become disturbed. You can become fatigued as a consequence and it becomes more difficult for you to cope with the demands of your day.

There are three types of insomnia. You might experience any one or all three of these types of sleep problems.

1. *Trouble going to sleep.* This is where you are unable to go to sleep despite being tired.
2. *Trouble staying asleep.* This is where you repeatedly wake throughout the night, but after a period of time, you are able to go back to sleep.
3. *Waking early and being unable to go back to sleep.* This where you wake early in the morning and, despite needing more sleep, you cannot return to sleep.

Each of these types of sleep problems is understandable if you take into consideration your stages of sleep.

Table 4: A description of the stages of sleep.

	Stages of sleep
Stage 1	This is a transitional stage from wakefulness to sleep. It is associated with very light sleep. During this stage, muscle activity slows down.
Stage 2	During this stage, your sleep starts to deepen. Your breathing pattern changes and slows as does your heart rate. Your body temperature drops slightly.
Stage 3	It is at this stage that deep sleep begins to be experienced. To signal the onset of deep sleep, your brain starts to generate slow delta waves.
Stage 4	This is when you are most deeply asleep. During this stage, your muscle activity is limited.
REM sleep	This refers to Rapid Eye Movement Sleep. It occurs when you are at the closest point to wakefulness. It is associated with vivid dreaming. During this stage, your heart rate increases.

Over the course of the night, you will cycle through these stages. For the first half or so of the night, you will cycle down into the deep sleep associated with stages 3 and 4. However, as the night progresses, the cycling pattern is lighter and does not involve deep sleep. This pattern is demonstrated in the diagram below. Periods of REM sleep occur at the point in the cycle when you are closest to waking.

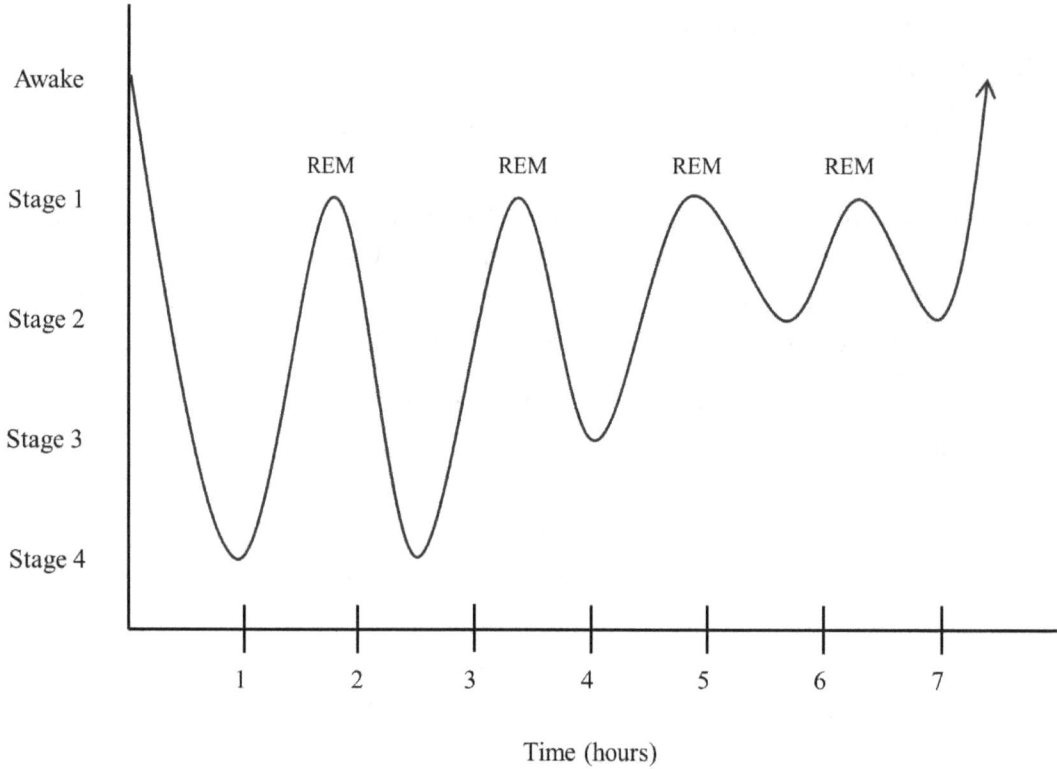

Figure 6: The cycles of sleep over the course of a sleep period.

When you have trouble falling asleep at the beginning of the night, you are struggling to enter into Stage 1 of sleep. This transitional stage is designed to pull you down into deeper sleep. Stage 1 allows you to do what your brain is inviting you to do, that is, go to sleep. Unfortunately, if you are stressed, your nervous system is generally too aroused to allow this to occur. Your nervous system fights against this natural urge to sleep. Your stressful thoughts are indicating to your brain that it is a good idea to stay awake in case something happens to which you need to respond.

When you have trouble staying asleep, you tend to wake up when your sleep cycle reaches those points where it is closest to wakefulness. In general, your nervous system is too aroused to allow you to stay asleep. Then, as soon as you wake, your mind turns to stressful thoughts that keep you awake until you can get back to sleep. This can happen many times throughout the night.

When you are troubled by waking early and being unable to return to sleep, this usually occurs in the second part of the night when you have moved past the deep sleep cycles. Your sleep is lighter, and when your nervous system is too aroused, and you come close to wakefulness, you become completely awake, your stressful thoughts begin, and you cannot get back to sleep.

What can I do about my internally generated sleep problems?

Each of these types of sleep disturbance can be influenced by racing thoughts. These thoughts are usually of a stressful nature. They increase your nervous system arousal, making it difficult to get any rest.

Here is a series of simple steps that should help you have a better night's sleep.

	Simple sleep strategy
1.	In the evening, avoid caffeine and sugary drinks and food.
2.	In the lead-up to your bedtime, start to wind down. Turn off stimulating television or stop engaging in other activities around the house that cause you to feel more alert.
3.	Have a small snack rich in carbohydrates.
4.	Get into a comfortable bed and into a comfortable position. Slow your breathing. Relax your muscle tension.
5.	Give your mind something to think about that is not emotionally arousing. This could be writing a simple story in your head, listing in your mind all the countries you can think of, starting with A, then B, etc. Count backwards by 7s from a randomly selected number.
6.	If your mind drifts to more stressful thoughts, acknowledge that is what is happening then return to the activity you chose to keep your mind focused.
7.	Allow yourself to drift off to sleep.

Worksheet available at elemen.com.au

The goal here is to create the right sort of internal environment to facilitate a good night's sleep. Avoid caffeine and sugary food or drinks because they can have a stimulating effect on your nervous system. In general, you should be aiming to 'turn off' by reducing the number of external stimulating activities. You do these things in preparation for sleep.

Carbohydrates can also increase your readiness for sleep. This is because carbohydrates contribute to an increase in your brain of a protein called tryptophan. This is a building block for a neurotransmitter called serotonin and a hormone called melatonin. Serotonin has a role in controlling sleep, appetite and mood. Melatonin release is triggered by darkness, and this hormone helps promote a regular sleep-wake cycle. This process, assisted by eating a carbohydrate-rich snack before bedtime, helps you sleep.

When your mind is already overrun by thoughts that are keeping you awake, it seems counterintuitive to give your brain something else to think about. However, it is not the thoughts themselves that will keep you awake. It is the nature of the thoughts that will have an effect on your sleep. In this way, you want to distract yourself from thinking stress-related thoughts, replacing them with thoughts that will not cause you to react emotionally. You should aim to keep your brain busy with mundane thoughts so that your mind is distracted from the stress-inducing thoughts. We like to refer to this activity as 'busy work' for your brain. It is the modern-day equivalent of counting sheep.

Mundane thoughts will allow you to drift off to sleep, whereas stress-related thoughts will keep you alert and awake. Your brain is always active so it is not possible to stop thinking. When you think of things that cause your nervous system to respond by increasing your arousal, you will have trouble sleeping. If you think calming or even boring thoughts, your brain will trigger the processes that lead you to falling asleep.

The same strategy of giving your mind something other than stressful things to think about can be applied if you awaken during the night. Simply get settled and focus on the mundane thoughts you have selected, allowing yourself to drift off back to sleep.

Learning to cope

The fact that you are struggling to deal with the stress associated with neighbourhood disputes makes it necessary to consider ways that might help you cope with what is happening. That is what we do when we are faced with problem situations in our lives… we try to use the skills we have to cope with our problems.

Coping

We all have our own coping resources and individual coping skills. Coping resources are the things we have available to help us cope, such as family and friends. Coping skills are the strategies we are good at that we use to deal with the problems we face. We have our own particular coping resources and specific coping skills because there is no one particular way of coping.

In a general sense, the way you will cope with a difficult neighbour will likely be a reflection of the way you have dealt with and solved other problems throughout your life. That is, the way you cope will reflect your general style of coping.

Your goal should be to understand how you cope and to make good use of the coping resources you have or can create, as well as the particular skills you have developed or can develop. This is true even if you take into account the fact that dealing with a difficult neighbour may be a more challenging problem than other problems you have usually faced. For those of you who feel they do not cope well with life problems, it may be the case you have been trying to develop coping skills based on a pattern of coping strategies that do not suit you.

To understand the way you cope and to use this knowledge to choose the best strategies to cope with a difficult neighbour, consideration needs to be given to the fundamental differences people can have in the way they approach problem situations. Let's look at the different approaches to coping so that you can work out your own preferred coping style.

Problem-focused coping vs. emotion-focused coping

To start, a distinction can be made between problem-focused coping strategies and emotion-focused strategies.

Who are problem-focused copers?

Problem-focused copers deal with their problems by considering the problem situation and looking for ways to solve it. They tend to want to *do* something when they are confronted with a problem. They are most comfortable when there are specific things related to the problem that can be the focus of their attention. In the context of a disagreement with a neighbour, problem-focused copers are the ones who will say, "Just tell me what I have to do to fix it", when they are dealing with a neighbour's difficult behaviour.

Who are emotion-focused copers?

Emotion-focused copers are the people who deal with their problems by expressing their emotional reactions to the situation. They will talk about the problem and cry when they feel the need. They see the value in looking to others to share their feelings about their problem. In the context of a dispute with a neighbour, the emotion-focused coper will want to talk about how the situation is making them feel.

Are people either emotion-focused or problem-focused copers?

Some people are strongly problem-focused copers, and some people are strongly emotion-focused copers. Others fall somewhere on the continuum between the two extreme positions. You may be more problem-focused than emotion-focused in your coping but still make use of some emotion-focused strategies… or the reverse.

You will be able to do a little exercise to find your coping preferences or to confirm them if you already have a good idea of where on the continuum you fall. But, first, we have to consider one other element.

Problem-approach vs. problem-avoidance coping

People assume that if we talk about coping strategies, they have to be good ones that will help us deal with the problems we face. This is not the case. People's coping styles can be divided on the basis of whether they tend to front up to their problems or whether they prefer to avoid them. This is the case for both problem-focused copers and emotion-focused copers.

Let's start by looking at problem-focused coping. How would problem approach and problem avoidance strategies differ? Consider the examples in the table below.

Table 5: Examples of problem-focused approach and avoidance strategies.

Problem-focused, problem approach strategies	Problem-focused, problem-avoidance strategies
Problem-solving Problem-solving coping strategies involve: - Examining the problem - Generating potential solutions - Evaluating the likelihood of a successful outcome - Moving forward and applying the strategy	*Problem avoidance* Problem avoidance coping strategies involve: - Deliberately avoiding thinking about the problem - Deliberately avoiding reminders of the problem
Cognitive restructuring Cognitive restructuring coping strategies involve: - Reframing your thoughts to think more reasonably about the problem - Correcting errors in thinking that are barriers to coping with the problem	*Wishful thinking* Wishful thinking as a coping strategy involves: - Wishing the problem would go away - Indulging in thoughts that things will return to 'normal' - Spending time thinking about how things will work out in your favour and as you wish

With regard to dealing with difficult neighbours, effective, problem-focused approach coping strategies may help in the following ways. They may help you think clearly about what needs to be done to resolve a problem situation. They can keep you focused on what you need to do without being overwhelmed by strong emotions. They can help you feel more in control.

Now, let's consider emotion-focused coping. The table below details examples of approach and avoidance emotion-focused coping strategies.

Table 6: Examples of emotion-focused approach and avoidance strategies.

Emotion-focused, problem approach strategies	Emotion-focused, problem-avoidance strategies
Emotion expression Emotion expression as a coping strategy involves: - Being open and talking about how you are feeling - Allowing yourself to experience your emotional reactions in relation to the problem - Using emotion expression as a form of catharsis, letting off steam to allow yourself to feel better for a while	*Self-criticism* Self-criticism as a coping strategy involves: - Blaming yourself for the problem - Criticising yourself for failing to control your emotional reaction to the problem - Viewing yourself as more generally deficient than is warranted
Social support Using social support as a coping strategy involves: - Turning to family and friends for support - Talking with your support network about how you are feeling - Taking comfort from your support people - Allowing your support network to offer instrumental support*	*Social withdrawal* Social withdrawal as a copy strategy involves: - Cutting yourself off from family and friends - Failing to seek professional support when it is needed - Refusing assistance offered by the people who wish to help you or would be willing to do so

* Instrumental support refers to the things people do to help you, such as cooking you meals or collecting your children from school.

When we consider dealing with a difficult neighbour, the effective emotion-focused approach coping strategies may be of assistance to you in a variety of ways. They can help you feel some relief when you feel overwhelmed by stress. They can help you take advantage of your support network of family and friends. They can help you deal with the emotional roller coaster ride of emotions that you experience with this situation.

Identifying your preferred coping style

The goal here is to identify the type of coping that works best for you. If you are an emotion-focused coper, you may see the value of a problem-focused coping approach, but it is unlikely that you could comfortably adopt problem-focused coping strategies and expect them to work for you. Your efforts would be better directed at taking advantage of your preferred style of coping and using problem-approach strategies.

Here is an exercise in determining what type of coping style best characterises your preferred type. Tick the boxes if you typically use the listed coping strategy.

	How do I normally cope?
Problem-solving	
	I work on finding ways to solve the problems I face.
	I work out what I should do, and then I follow the plan.
	I like to work out a plan and then move forward.
	I believe there is a solution to every problem.
Problem avoidance	
	I try to act like nothing is wrong.
	When faced with a problem, I choose not to do anything, even when I know I should.
	I try not to spend any time thinking about the problem.
	When the problem comes to mind, I push it out of my head.
Cognitive restructuring	
	I think about my problems in a way that allows me to realise I can manage them.
	I think about the problem to change the way I react to it.
	I try to look on the bright side of any situation.
	I try to put things into perspective.

Wishful thinking	
	When faced with a problem, I just wish it would go away.
	I just hope a miracle will happen to make everything all right.
	I hope the problem will fix itself.
	I wish that someone would come and fix the problem for me.
Emotion expression	
	When faced with a problem, I allow myself to express my feelings about it.
	I do not try to bottle up my feelings; I let them go so that I can feel better.
	I do not hide my feelings about the problem from other people.
	When faced with a problem, I just need some time to experience my feelings.
Self-criticism	
	I blame myself for the problem I am facing.
	I ask myself what I have done to make the problem happen.
	I tend to hold myself responsible for the problems I face.
	When a problem occurs, I feel I should have done things differently.
Social support	
	I turn to the people I know will listen when I talk about how I feel.
	I feel better when I can talk to others about my problems.
	When faced with a problem, I seek advice from people I trust.
	I allow other people to offer help and support when I am dealing with a problem.

	Social withdrawal
	When faced with a problem, I like to avoid other people and spend time by myself.
	When I am struggling with a problem, I do not want to be around other people.
	I do not share my thoughts and feelings with others.
	I do not accept the help others offer.

Checklist available at elemen.com.au

What type of coper are you? Add up the ticks you have placed in each of the categories and enter the number in the following table.

Ways of coping scoring sheet	
Problem-focused strategies	*Emotion-focused strategies*
_____ Problem-solving _____ Cognitive restructuring _____ Problem avoidance _____ Wishful thinking _____ Total	_____ Emotion expression _____ Social support _____ Self-criticism _____ Social withdrawal _____ Total
Problem-approach strategies	*Problem-avoidance strategies*
_____ Problem-solving _____ Cognitive restructuring _____ Emotion expression _____ Social support _____ Total	_____ Problem-avoidance _____ Wishful thinking _____ Self-criticism _____ Social withdrawal _____ Total

Score sheet available at elemen.com.au

When comparing your problem-focused and emotion-focused strategies, see where you have scored the highest. This may show a strong preference for one type of coping strategy or the other. If so, you can build on your preferred coping type when you consider what coping strategies will help you with your current situation. If you have similar totals for both problem-focused and emotion-focused strategies, you would do best to include each type in your coping plan.

When considering whether you use problem-approach strategies or problem-avoidance strategies, you are considering whether adjustments have to be made in the way you cope. If you predominantly use problem-avoidance strategies, you can learn to abandon those in favour of problem-approach strategies while staying within the same style of coping strategy, that is, problem-focused or emotion-focused.

Using effective coping strategies

We have already covered information about coping preferences and coping strategies, both good ones and ones that do not work very effectively. We are now going to consider how to take full advantage of your ways of coping, building on problem-approach strategies and letting go of problem-avoidance strategies.

Building your coping repertoire

As you now better understand the ways you cope, you can start to build a plan of how you are going to move forward, adopting coping strategies that work for you. Let's consider some examples of coping strategies you could adopt.

Problem-focused strategies

We will start by looking at problem-solving strategies. Here you are trying to work out a plan of how you would go about solving a specific problem situation, followed by decision-making with regard to which potential solution you would choose. You then should be able to follow through and solve your problem.

Let's consider an example of this process.

Example of a problem-solving strategy
What is the problem? Clearly define the problem you are facing. *The property beyond my back fence is unsightly, and I cannot avoid seeing it when I am on the terrace in my backyard. Their yard is a jungle, and the paint is peeling off their house. It causes me to enjoy my garden less than I would like.*
Generate as many possible solutions as you can. List the ones that are likely to work. *I could do the following:*   *I could do nothing and put up with it.*   *I could complain to the local council and then wait and see what happens.*   *I could plant a row of trees to block out the view.*   *I could put some lattice on top of the back fence and plant an attractive, quick-growing climber to block the view.*

Consider the likelihood of each of these strategies being successful.

The likely outcomes are:

> *If I do nothing and try to put up with it, I doubt that I would be able to do so. Every time I went outside, I would see into their property and I would be reminded of how much it aggravates me. Also, the impact on the outlook of my yard would remain unchanged and I would be less likely to invite people around because it makes my property look unattractive as well.*

> *If I complained to the local council about the state of the property, there is no guarantee that anything would change. Even if the council told them to clean up the mess, it could still take ages for anything to happen. In the meantime, I would still have the same outlook from my terrace. Also, if I made a complaint, it is possible that the neighbours would then become hostile, and it could become uncomfortable for me as a result.*

> *If I planted a row of trees, they would eventually block the view of the neighbour's property. However, I could not afford to plant mature trees. If I planted smaller trees that I could afford, they would take ages to grow to a height that would make any difference to the view.*

If I put some lattice along the top of the back fence, it would reduce the visibility into the next property. By planting a quick growing climber, my view of the neighbour's property would be completely blocked. It would also make the back of my garden look very nice.

Select the problem-solving strategy that is likely to work the best.

I think I will choose to put some lattice on the fence and plant something to block the view. This is an affordable option and, importantly, it could be done quite quickly so I would soon have the outcome I want, that is, not being able to see into my neighbour's property.

What are you going to do next?

I am going to start measuring the fence and checking out the price of lattice. I will have a chat with the people at the local garden nursery to see what options there are for a quick growing and attractive climbing plant.

In this example, the person has thought about the problem and identified possible options for resolving it. The person then considered what the likely outcome for each possible solution would be. They then chose their preferred solution and worked out a plan for their next step. This is a good problem-solving approach.

Below is a worksheet you can use for problem-solving coping strategies.

Problem-solving strategy worksheet
What is the problem? Clearly define the problem you are facing.
Generate as many possible solutions as you can. List the ones that are likely to work.
Consider the likelihood of each of these strategies being successful.
Select the problem-solving strategy that is likely to work the best.
What are you going to do next?

Worksheet available at elemen.com.au

Now, let's consider a cognitive restructuring approach to coping. Cognitive restructuring refers to changing the way you think about a problem. Below is an example of a cognitive restructuring approach to addressing a problem situation.

Example of a cognitive restructuring strategy
What is the problem? *I had a discussion with my new neighbours about the exact boundary between our two properties. They thought that part of my fence was on their property. It was stressful for me because I had experienced a similar dispute at a property I owned previously that had become quite heated.*
What are you thinking? *Not again. This is going to turn out badly. Things will become so hostile that I might have to move.*
What evidence do you have that this is true? *None, really. Even though there had been a problem before, there is no evidence that it will be like that again.*
What evidence do you have against this being true? *The discussion I had with my new neighbours was quite civil. They seemed open to the idea that the boundary was not as they thought. I have seen no other sign that the neighbours are anything other than reasonable people.*
Even if it was true, what is the worst thing that would happen? *Even if it was true that a part of the fence is slightly on their property, the worst thing that would happen is that we will move the fence.*
What do you conclude? *I realised I was becoming stressed because of my past experience. There is nothing to say this experience would turn out the same. These neighbours are not the same as my previous neighbours, and I now know a lot more about boundaries between properties, so I am in a better position to negotiate.*

Here, the person in this example challenged the way they were thinking about their situation. Then, they examined whether the situation was as bad as they were interpreting it to be. Having realised that was not the case, they then worked out a better and more realistic way of thinking about their problem. You can see that their alternative thoughts about their situation would make them feel better. They had become stressed because of their past experience. By working through the situation, they were able to see that they had overreacted to a reasonable enquiry from the new neighbour.

Below is a worksheet you can use for cognitive restructuring strategies.

Cognitive restructuring strategy worksheet
What is the problem?
What are you thinking?
What evidence do you have that this is true?
What evidence do you have against this being true?
Even if it was true, what is the worst thing that would happen?
What do you conclude?

Worksheet available at elemen.com.au

Emotion-focused strategies

Next, we will consider how to enhance your emotion expression coping skills.

Example of an emotion expression strategy
What is the problem?   *I was having problems with my neighbour, but I didn't want anyone to think I was the sort of person who couldn't get along with their neighbours.*
What did you do?   *I chose not to tell anyone about what my neighbours had been doing that was making me so stressed.*
What were the advantages of doing this?   *I suppose the advantage is that people wouldn't form an opinion about me because of what was happening in my life... although I don't know for certain that they would think negatively about me.*
What were the disadvantages of doing this?   *The downside of saying nothing is that I had no opportunity to get things off my chest. This made me feel even more stressed than I might have felt otherwise. I felt like I was carrying this huge burden that I couldn't talk about.*
What could you have done differently?   *I could have chosen a friend or a family member I trusted and who knew me well and would listen to my concerns about what had been happening. I could have created this opportunity to just talk about how I was feeling.*
What would the advantages have been of doing things this other way?   *I would have felt relieved to talk about how I was feeling. I think I could have let go of some of my stress if I was just able to talk about things.*
Would there have been any disadvantage of doing things this other way?   *Not that I can think of. I would choose to talk to a friend or family member that I trusted and who normally would support me. So, I believe that, no matter what I say about the matter, the person I chose would not think badly of me.*

> What will you do next time you feel like this?
>
> *Next time I feel this stressed, I will speak up about how my problem is making me feel. Next time, I will not allow the stress to build up like it did this time.*

In this case, the person went through a process of examining the pros and cons associated with the decision they made to not talk about how they were feeling regarding their problem with their neighbour. They recognised that this had prevented them from genuinely expressing their emotions in a way that would have been a relief for them. The conclusion was reached that the better option was to allow themselves to express how they had been feeling to someone who would listen to what they had to say.

Below is a worksheet for emotion expression strategies.

Emotion expression strategy worksheet
What is the problem?
What did you do?
What were the advantages of doing this?
What were the disadvantages of doing this?
What could you have done differently?

What would the advantages have been of doing things this other way?
Would there have been any disadvantage of doing things this other way?
What will you do next time you feel like this?

Worksheet available at elemen.com.au

Finally, we can consider how to use social support as a coping strategy.

Example of social support as a strategy
What is the problem? *I am being harassed by a neighbour and I don't know what to do about it. I have never been in this situation before and I have no clue what to do to try and fix the problem.*
What have you done in response to this problem? *I have tried and tried to come up with a plan of what to do. I have laid awake at night. I have spent a lot of time thinking about the problem and about my neighbour, but I haven't come up with anything. Also, I know I am too stressed. It is making me feel unwell. But all I have been doing is worrying about that, too.*
How has responding in this way helped you with your problem? *It hasn't helped at all. I haven't solved the problem with my neighbour and I can't seem to help myself feel any better.*
What could you do instead? *I could reach out to family and friends to seek their support and advice.*

How would this be likely to work out?
I have some people in my life who usually give me really good advice and always give me lots of support. They would be able to look at the problem from a different perspective so they are likely to be able to see solutions that I might not be able to see.
So, what are you going to do next?
Next time I feel like this, I am going to call a friend or a member of my family and ask them what they would suggest I do to fix the problem, and I will seek some support with regard to my stress level.

Here, the person thought through their situation and realised there were potential solutions available to them and there were advantages to pursuing the solution. It was an easy step then to follow through with their plan and reach out to others.

Below is a worksheet you can use for social support strategies.

Social support as a strategy worksheet
What is the problem?
What have you done in response to this problem?
How has responding in this way helped you with your problem?
What could you do instead?
How would this be likely to work out?

So, what are you going to do next?

Worksheet available at elemen.com.au

In moving forward, remember to choose the coping strategies that best suit your preferred coping style. Always choose approach strategies rather than avoidance strategies, no matter what your coping style.

Learning to think clearly

So far in this workbook, we have indicated that the way we think about the things we experience influences how we react to them. We touched on this when we examined ways to regulate your emotions and learned to control angry feelings, in particular. To feel better, we might have to change the way we view something so that we are not vulnerable to distressed reactions. Let's now consider ways we can challenge unhelpful thinking and replace it with the types of thoughts that allow us to see things more clearly and choose behaviours that will help us.

How are our thoughts affected?

As we go through life, we can develop unhelpful thinking styles or errors in our thinking. These errors influence how we interpret the world around us and how we fit into that world. In an attempt to make sense of the world, we develop 'templates' or models of how we think things should work.

For example, you might develop a template that tells you that to be a worthwhile person, everyone should like you. On the surface, this seems workable. It is nice when people like you, and it makes you feel good, including feeling good about yourself. However, if you have a template that you are worthwhile only if everyone likes you, what happens if, for some reason, someone chooses not to like you? You then become upset about something that really is an ordinary enough experience. You then feel like you are not worthwhile, even in situations where the fact that the other person does not like you says more about them than it does about you.

We have found that people choose not to like others for the oddest of reasons. For example, one person disclosed that they found they could not like people who even vaguely looked like a cousin they did not admire. Should your feelings of self-worth be affected by the fact that you look somewhat like a person you have never met? It is obvious that the answer is no. Unfortunately, your template might tell you that to be a worthwhile person, *everyone* has to like you. You can see the problem.

Our individual templates are put together based on information from a variety of sources, including, for example, our personality and our experiences throughout life. If the messages we receive from our experiences in life are good and healthy ones, we tend to have good and healthy templates of how the world works and how we fit into that world. However, if the messages are distorted in some way (e.g., being told you have to be the best at everything you do, that no one will like you if you disagree with them, your needs are not as important as other people's needs), then the template we develop will reflect these messages and will be unhelpful.

Core beliefs

So, how does this template affect us? It tells us how we should respond when dealing with our world and the people in it. The information we gather determines our 'core beliefs' about three things:

> How safe or dangerous we perceive the world to be.
>
> Our place in that world and our value as a person.
>
> How certain the future feels.

These core beliefs are not the 'truth' of things. They develop as a result of the information we gather along the way in life, whether or not that information is helpful or unhelpful, clear or confusing, or accurate or distorted.

If we have helpful, clear and accurate templates, then our core beliefs are healthy, and our thinking does not contain errors about how the world works and how we fit into that world. However, if we have unhelpful, confusing and distorted templates, our thinking contains errors that affect how we react to the world and how we view ourselves in that world.

Cognitive errors

Cognitive errors are the errors in thinking that occur when our templates of how the world works and how we fit into that world send us the wrong message. Our thinking about our experiences is then altered by the wrong message. Problems arise when we engage in certain types of cognitive errors.

Below are some of the most common cognitive errors. As you read through them, think about whether these types of errors occur in your thinking.

Table 7: Descriptions of the common errors in thinking.

Types of errors in thinking	
Error type	*Error in thinking*
Filtering	A person whose thinking is affected by filtering takes the negative details of an event and magnifies those details while filtering out all positive aspects of the situation. For example, a person may have hostile feelings towards a neighbour who did one thing to annoy them because they filter out all the information they have about how their neighbour is otherwise a good person.

Polarised thinking	With polarised thinking, things are either 'black or white' or 'all or nothing'. People who think this way place situations in 'either/or' categories, with no middle ground to account for the complexity of most situations. For example, a person may view the neighbours around them as either good or bad, friends or enemies.
Overgeneralisation	A person comes to a general conclusion based on a single incident or a single piece of evidence. If something bad happens just once, they expect it to happen over and over again. For example, a person may believe they are always going to have a poor relationship with their neighbour because of one unfortunate dispute.
Jumping to conclusions	A person who jumps to conclusions 'knows' what the other person is thinking about without that person saying so. For example, a person may be certain that a neighbour will complain about something they have done on their own property without any sign that is likely to happen.
Catastrophising	A person who catastrophises expects disaster to strike, no matter what. A person hears about a problem and uses *what-if* questions to imagine the worst outcome. For example, a person may worry that a dispute will never be resolved, and they will be forced to live next to people who 'hate' them.
Personalisation	A person believes that everything others do or say is some kind of direct, personal reaction to them. They take everything personally. For example, a person may feel that a neighbour does not like them personally despite the fact that they are not friendly with anyone in the neighbourhood.
Control fallacies	This distortion involves two different but related beliefs about being in complete control of every situation. That might be external control, where the person feels they are a helpless victim of fate, or internal control, where a person assumes responsibility for the pain and unhappiness of others. For example, a person may believe they have to put up with poor behaviour from a neighbour because things never work out in their favour and the 'world' never takes their side.

Fallacy of fairness	A person feels resentful because they think that they know what is fair, but other people will not agree with them. People who go through life applying a measuring ruler against every situation, judging its 'fairness', will often feel resentful, angry and hopeless. For example, a person may find it more difficult to have a disagreement with a neighbour because they are always good to their neighbours, so they believe the neighbours should be good to them, no matter the circumstances.
Blaming	This person holds other people responsible for their own emotional pain. Alternatively, they may blame themselves for every problem – even those clearly outside their control. For example, a person may hold a neighbour responsible for their general unhappiness.
Shoulds	Should statements (e.g., I should visit my parents more) appear as a list of ironclad rules about how every person should behave. Breaking these rules makes a person angry. They also feel guilty when they violate their own rules. For example, a person may have a list of things their neighbours should and must do to be good community members.
Emotional reasoning	This distortion can be summed up by the statement, "If I feel that way, it must be true". Whatever a person is feeling is believed to be true, automatically and unconditionally. If a person feels stupid and boring, then they must be stupid and boring. Emotional reasoning stops a person from thinking rationally and logically. For example, a person may believe their neighbour has definitely done the wrong thing solely on the basis that they are unhappy with the neighbour's actions.
Fallacy of change	A person expects that other people will change to suit them if they just pressure or cajole them enough. A person needs to change people because their hopes for success and happiness seem to depend entirely on them. For example, a person may believe they can force their neighbour to behave differently if they just put enough pressure on them. They believe they cannot be happy unless the neighbour's behaviour changes.

Global labelling	A person generalises one or two qualities into a negative global judgment about themselves or another person. This is an extreme form of overgeneralising. Instead of describing an error in the context of a specific situation, a person will attach an unhealthy universal label to themselves or others. For example, a person may label their neighbour a bad person even though they had just mistakenly done one thing wrong.
Always being right	When a person engages in this error of thinking, they are continually putting other people on trial to prove that their own opinions and actions are the absolutely correct ones. To a person engaging in 'always being right', being wrong is unthinkable – they will go to great lengths to demonstrate their rightness. For example, a person who thinks they are right is unlikely to easily reach a compromise in relation to a dispute with a neighbour.
Heaven's reward fallacy	This is a false belief that a person's sacrifice and self-denial will eventually pay off as if some global force is keeping score. This is a variation of the fallacy of fairness because, in a fair world, the people who work the hardest will get the largest reward. For example, a person may be confused about a neighbour treating them with disregard because they always go out of their way to help others and be a good person.

Let's consider how these errors in thinking affect a person's point of view. Below are examples of these types of logical errors in thinking, along with a more rational point of view.

Table 8: Examples of rational and irrational perspectives for each error in thinking.

Correcting your thinking	
Error in thinking	*A rational view*
Filtering	
Joel have been living next door to a neighbour for a number of years. In general, their relationship had been a reasonably good one. They had helped each other out on occasions and their children had played together. Although they were not close friends, Joe had positive regard for them. One day, Joel's neighbour lit a fire in his backyard to burn a pile of leaves he raked up. The fire burned out of control and set fire to the fence and a tree on Joel's property. The fire was quickly brought under control and extinguished. From that point on, Joel thought his neighbour was a fool, and their relationship deteriorated. He interpreted everything he did as lacking in skill and forethought. Joel forgot that, apart from this accident, he had always regarded his neighbour in a positive way.	Joel was making the mistake of filtering out everything he had always known about his neighbour and replacing it with a more negative view that was based solely on one mistake his neighbour had made. Joel would have been better off seeing this mistake in the context of years of good neighbourly behaviour. Accidents happen. Joel could have seen that it was not his neighbour's intention to set fire to the fence. By doing so, Joel would have saved himself from the negative feelings he was having, that were going to affect his relationship with his neighbour in the future.

Polarised thinking	
Sean lived in a complex of six villa units. Sean had a friendly relationship with four of his neighbours but he did not like the other two. The people who lived in these two units liked their privacy and were not overtly friendly. Sean viewed their reticence to engage in friendly banter as evidence that they were not to the trusted. One day, when Sean's neighbour drove into their car parking space, they failed to see Sean. They walked inside their unit without acknowledging him. Sean was infuriated by their behaviour. He felt disrespected. He told his friends that, he supposed, he could expect little else considering those people were always rude.	Sean expended a lot of emotional energy deciding who his friends were and who they were not. However, if you asked him, he could not give clear examples of why some people were not on his list of good people. It is interesting that, for all the emotional energy he expended on the matter, his neighbours not on the 'good list' were unaware of his feelings and unaffected by them. So, in effect, Sean was the person who was making himself unhappy. He would have been better off seeing that people often have a combination of positive and less positive attributes. Also, it would be sensible for Sean to see that he did not have to be friendly with everyone and that it was all right to let other people live the lives they wanted.

Overgeneralisation	
Sonya and her neighbour had a disagreement about the replacement of a fence. They were both jointly responsible for covering the cost. Sonya wanted one particular type of fencing that was consistent with the fences along her other boundaries. Her neighbour wanted to replace the fence with materials that were consistent with the fencing of their boundaries. The old fence was still there because they could not agree about the replacement. Sonya and another neighbour organised a community meeting about some issues they wanted to present to the council in their area and some other plans they had to make their neighbourhood safer and more child-friendly. Sonya made a point of not inviting her neighbour with whom she was having a disagreement about the fence to attend the meeting. Sonya's view was that because they disagreed about the fence, they were going to disagree about everything, and the neighbour's presence at the community meeting would not help advance their plans.	Sonya would have done well to consider that one disagreement that was relatively contained to a specific issue would be unlikely to have any bearing on other issues, especially as there had been no other disagreements or difficulties with this neighbour in the past. Rather than this one disagreement reflecting an overall pattern of obstruction on the part of the neighbour, it probably demonstrated nothing more than an understandable desire by both parties to have their own backyards looking nice.

Jumping to conclusions

Olivia had plans to put a pool in her backyard. She was aware that this was going to cause some noise when the location for the pool was excavated. However, the pool company informed Olivia that, barring unforeseen difficulties, the excavation could be done quickly. Nevertheless, Olivia was certain that her neighbour would complain about the noise and make it difficult for her to get her plan for the pool approved. She did not know her neighbour very well and rarely had anything to do with them. However, she was convinced they were going to thwart her plans.	Without any evidence that this was the case, Olivia believed she knew how her neighbour would react. She was becoming stressed and feeling hostile towards the neighbour despite them not even knowing yet of her intention to put in a pool. Olivia would have been better off relying on objective facts to which she had access. Namely, the excavation noise would likely be over within a couple of hours, the council permitted such noise in general terms, and she had not had any disagreement with her neighbours about any other issue. It was serving Olivia no good purpose to believe she knew how her neighbour would react, and it was making her stressed without cause.

Catastrophising	
Gemma's neighbour wanted to subdivide their large property and sell off one section, making it available for the construction of another house. Gemma did not like the idea because it would require a right-of-way driveway to be put in to reach the new house to be built behind the neighbour's existing house. Gemma did not like the idea of cars driving along beside her fence, believing that the traffic would interfere with her enjoyment of the garden behind her own home. From Gemma's perspective, the changes would mean a constant flow of traffic to and from the house to be constructed. She believed that this would lead to bad feelings between herself and both her existing neighbour and the people who would move into the proposed new house. She anticipated either years of hostility or she would have to move, which she did not want to do.	In reality, it is unlikely that Gemma would experience an endless flow of traffic, as she feared. In any other way, the subdivision and the construction would be unlikely to have any impact on Gemma beyond the owner's vehicle using the proposed new driveway. Indeed, the changes would be more likely to have a greater impact on her neighbour, who would have to forfeit part of their front block of land for a right-of-way driveway. Also, there was no real evidence that Gemma would be facing years of hostile feelings. Although she might feel bitter for a while if the plans went ahead, in all likelihood, the actual impact would allow Gemma to get used to the change and not think about it much anymore. Gemma would have done better to consider ways to protect herself from the activity on the driveway, such as noise-reducing foliage or fencing, if that became necessary, rather than making herself stressed about something she did not yet even know was going to be a problem.

Personalisation	
Leah and Robbie lived on a street where most of their neighbours were friendly and socialised together regularly. This was true of all their neighbours except for one. The people who lived in the house next door to Leah and Robbie were not interested in participating in social events and liked to maintain their privacy. They were civil to the other people in the street but did not seek out interactions with them. Leah was upset. She just could not figure out why these neighbours disliked her so much. She raised the issue with Robbie all the time. She said she could not think of anything she had done to offend them, and she felt disgruntled that they had failed to respond to her friendly overtures.	Leah was making the mistake of assuming that the reaction of these neighbours targeted her. In looking for explanations for their unfriendliness, she was examining her own behaviour and becoming confused when she could find no reason for their lack of friendly response. Leah would have done well to take a step back and look at the big picture. If she had done so, she would have seen that the neighbours were not targeting her. Rather, they treated everyone in the street in the same way. She might then have understood that they were people who enjoyed their privacy rather than believing they were responding to something Leah had done.
Control fallacies	
Warren's neighbours were trespassing on his land and it was upsetting him. Rather than walk a short distance to join a walking path behind both their properties, the neighbours just jumped the fence and walked through Warren's garden to join the path. These neighbours were damaging his flowerbed and invading his privacy. However, Warren was reluctant to do anything about it. He saw himself as unlucky in life. Nothing ever seemed to go his way. He believed there was no point in trying to fight this matter with his neighbour because the same forces that had affected him before in his life would affect him again. He believed he would not be able to stop them, and they would be allowed to do as they wished on his property.	With Warren holding the view that he was just a hapless victim of a system that does not support him, he has made the decision to do nothing. This is despite the fact that his neighbour is entering his property uninvited and damaging his garden. Because he believes that he has no control over how the world treats him, he has made no effort to exert any influence on how things would work out for him. Doing nothing is causing him stress. He would be better off realising that he does have some rights and exploring whether what the neighbour is doing was illegal. He could then identify the appropriate avenues to make it stop happening. If he is successful, it will encourage him to be more assertive in the future if someone clearly is taking advantage of him.

Fallacy of fairness

Brendan was the sort of person who went out of his way to help his neighbours. He said he was happy to help and did not expect anything in return. Also, Brendan was very careful about how his behaviour affected others. Before doing anything around his garden, he considered whether his actions were likely to affect his neighbours. He never played music loudly and never threw parties.

Recently, Brendan had become quite confused about his neighbour's behaviour. Brendan's neighbour had let his garden become overgrown, and the seeds from the noxious weeds that had sprung up were blowing into Brendan's garden and infiltrating his garden bed. The time Brendan spent in the garden to keep on top of this problem significantly increased. Brendan spoke with the neighbour and asked whether he could do something about the state of his garden because of the effect it was having on his own garden. The neighbour said he was not interested in gardening and that the problems Brendan was having in his own garden were his responsibility to solve and not the neighbour's responsibility.

Brendan was hurt and angry about his neighbour's disregard for his concerns. Brendan believed that because he had acted fairly with his neighbours, they should act fairly with him. Brendan has made a mistake in believing that his understanding of fairness will determine how other people will behave. Although Brendan may choose to act reasonably with his neighbour because of the standards he sets for his own behaviour, others will choose how they wish to conduct themselves.

Blaming

Things were not going very well for Audrey. Her marriage had ended, and it had become necessary for her to move from the home she loved to a house she did not particularly like. She was having some problems at work, and some of her relationships with friends had been affected by her divorce. In general, Audrey was feeling stressed and unhappy.

To top things off, Audrey's neighbours' dog regularly escaped from their yard and would come onto Audrey's property and dig up her garden. She spoke to the neighbours about their dog, and the neighbours apologised. They said they had nicknamed the dog 'Houdini' because of its tendency to escape. They suggested that Audrey just let them know when the dog was in her yard, and they would come and get it. This was not an adequate solution for Audrey because the dog kept coming into her yard and digging up the garden before she noticed what it was doing. Interactions between Audrey and her neighbours deteriorated. Audrey blamed them for making her so unhappy. She attributed all her negative emotions to the 'refusal' of her neighbours to contain their pet.

Audrey was blaming her neighbours for all of her unhappiness despite them only being involved in one issue. By doing so, this was causing Audrey to do nothing about the other aspects of her life that were causing her distress. As far as Audrey was concerned, the only way she could be happy was if her neighbours controlled their dog. Audrey would have been better off considering the bigger picture of her life. Although her neighbours were responsible for one issue that was upsetting her, they were not responsible for the stressed state Audrey was in, which probably affected how strongly Audrey was reacting to the dog issue. Audrey could have been working on her emotional state and quality of life separately from the issue of a dog who sometimes dug a hole in her garden.

Shoulds	
Dylan had rules about how the world should work and how things should be. He had a specific set of rules about how neighbours should behave. The rules were extensive. Lawns should be regularly mowed. Mailboxes should be emptied regularly so that brochures and catalogues did not build up. Newspapers needed to be collected within a reasonable timeframe. Garden edges should be trimmed. Maintenance of the external aspects of the house should be regularly attended to and concrete driveways should be pressured washed. Dylan's neighbours on one side of his property did not care about any of the things that were important to Dylan. They had a much more easy-going approach to life and thought these things were not worth worrying about. This difference in attitude led to many angry interactions between Dylan and his neighbour. Dylan kept telling them what they should be doing. The neighbour kept telling Dylan to 'chill out'.	Dylan was making the mistake of believing that others should agree with what he considered to be important. He could not understand why his neighbour was not interested in doing things that Dylan thought he must do. The trouble is that Dylan was making imperative demands about matters that, in effect, are a matter of choice. Dylan would have been better off realising that, while it was his preference to conduct himself in a particular way, it may be the preference of others to do things differently. By doing this, Dylan would be able to focus on his own choices and not be upset by his neighbour's choices.

Emotional reasoning	
Colin liked peace and quiet. As far as he was concerned, the quieter the better. Therefore, it was disturbing for Colin when he found out that the new neighbours had young children. Colin was concerned that his peaceful existence was going to be disturbed by the noise children would inevitably make. After moving in, the neighbour's children did play in their backyard under the supervision of their parents. By other people's standards, the children did not make much noise. However, Colin reacted poorly to their normal play. He was furious that he had to put up with the noise. He believed his neighbours had no right to create such a disturbance in the neighbourhood. He considered the behaviour of the children to be unacceptable and the quality of his neighbours' parenting skills to be appalling. As a result, Colin started a campaign to have the neighbours, who rented the property, evicted.	The intensity of Colin's response caused him to interpret the children's behaviour and the parents' decision to allow them to play in the backyard as unacceptable, inappropriate, and just plain wrong. Because he preferred peace and quiet, and his reaction to the sound of children playing was severe, he believed the problem was so severe that he should not have to tolerate it. He then made a choice, in effect, to cause harm to his neighbours by working to have them evicted. It would have been more reasonable for Colin to learn to deal with his noise intolerance and manage his stress. He might then be able to see that what he was complaining about was, in fact, quite normal neighbourhood behaviour, and it was his emotional reaction that caused him to view it otherwise.

Fallacy of change

Paul was only happy when things were the way he wanted them to be. He was a member of a community group that raised money for projects in their neighbourhood. He had clear ideas about what direction the group should take with regard to their activities. Paul was clashing with some other members of the community group. Although committed to the group's goals, the other members took a more relaxed approach to the activities the group undertook and liked to take the time to enjoy the social aspects of the group meetings. Also, the things they saw as worth pursuing were not the same as those Paul saw as important. To try to bring the group members into line with how he thought they should behave, Paul made incessant demands, berated group members for behaviours that were not directly goal-oriented and insisted on 'holding the floor' at any meeting. Paul believed that if he just forced the members to stay focused, he would have the group working in the way he wanted.	Paul has made the mistake of assuming that because he values certain things highly, everyone else should value them in the same way. And he thought the best way to make that happen was to push and push until everyone else came into line with his views. He assumes that everyone else should change to suit him rather than accommodate the needs of the majority. By pushing to get his way, Paul was probably creating a situation where the others were less likely to listen to his views and more likely to reject his plans than the reverse. Paul was creating a situation that had the potential for increasing levels of conflict for himself. He would have been better off understanding the importance of compromise. He would have had an easier time if he at least considered other people's points of view rather than trying to force them to do as he said.

Global labelling

On one occasion, Larry had mentioned to his neighbour that the tree his neighbour's children were climbing in was not stable and was likely to drop its branches unexpectedly. Larry knew a lot about trees and thought his neighbour should heed his warning. However, from time to time, the children would climb into the tree despite Larry's warning. One afternoon, months after Larry warned his neighbour about the tree, one of the neighbour's children slipped while climbing the tree, fell to the ground and broke her collarbone. Larry was outraged about what he saw as the neighbour's irresponsibility. He told other neighbours in the street that his neighbour was an abusive parent by allowing the child to climb the tree after receiving Larry's warning, despite the fact that the child fell because she slipped rather than a tree branch breaking. Larry refused to have anything to do with his neighbour because, he reasoned, he was now aware of what a terrible person his neighbour was.	The view Larry was taking of a simple accident was influencing how he saw his neighbour in a global sense. This effect was so strong that Larry was vilifying his neighbour to others in the neighbourhood. Larry would have been better off avoiding labelling his neighbour as an abusive parent on the basis of an accident. It is likely that there would be some people who would disapprove of these types of opinions being shared, and Larry could find himself losing the positive regard of others in his neighbourhood.

Always being right

Dorothy was a confident person who believed she was right in her views. Dorothy was required to enter into a neighbourhood dispute resolution process. There had been a dispute with a neighbour about the cost of repairing some damage that Dorothy accused her neighbour of causing, although her neighbour denied responsibility. Even though there was no strong evidence that the neighbour had caused the damage, Dorothy sought a legal resolution in her favour. The court decided that it was unlikely that the matter could be found in Dorothy's favour, but Dorothy made it clear that she would not accept this decision and would take the matter further. By entering into this legal process, Dorothy was told that it was necessary to engage in a dispute resolution process with a trained mediator.

Unfortunately, no progress was being made in this process. Dorothy was certain that she was right and, therefore, should win. The neighbour was offering to assist in the restoration of the damage, despite it not being determined to be the neighbour's fault, but the neighbour was unwilling to cover the entire cost. Dorothy thought the suggestion was unacceptable. Dorothy believed she was right in her views and would settle for nothing but an outcome entirely in her favour.

By being driven by a need to be right about this, and many other things for that matter, Dorothy was creating a problem for herself. She could not see that partial success was better than no success at all. She would have been better off listening to the advice the court had given her and accepting the assistance of the mediator to obtain the best possible outcome… that might not be entirely the outcome she wanted. Certainly, by doing this, her chances of some degree of satisfaction would have been significantly enhanced.

Heaven's reward fallacy

Chloe always put other people's needs before her own. She ran around after people, listened to their problems, and looked after their children and their pets. Because of her kindness, people often responded warmly to Chloe. Their gratitude encouraged Chloe to continue to help others because she knew that she was making a difference by helping them. Then Chloe's world came crashing down. An issue had arisen that caused an argument between Chloe and her neighbour. Choe could not understand why the neighbour was being so hostile. But what surprised Chloe the most was the fact that when she turned to her friends for support, they seemed to take the side of the neighbour in this matter, and they encouraged her to see that the neighbour had not done anything inappropriate and, in general, the problem was not worth worrying about. Chloe was devastated by the lack of support she received after she had helped so many of these people in the past.	Chloe made the mistake of believing that because she had done much to help others, they would unconditionally support her when she needed that support. She had assumed that this would be her reward for all the good Samaritan work she had undertaken to make other people's lives easier. Chloe would have been better off understanding that, while she is in charge of her own choices, other people will make up their own minds about how they behave. These people would be unlikely to be keeping score of what the world 'owed' Chloe for all her good work. Also, it would help her to see that even if these people did not support her with regard to this particular issue, it did not follow that they are less appreciative of her kindnesses

It is apparent that these types of logical errors do not make things easy for us. Quite the opposite. They lead us to misinterpret events so that we adopt a limited or negative perspective that colours how we view things, our emotional responses, and the choices of how we behave as a consequence.

Why do we think in unhelpful ways?

Where do unhelpful thinking styles comes from? To answer this question, we have to learn more about the theory of cognitive behaviour therapy (CBT). According to the cognitive model, there are different levels of thought. This is displayed in the diagram below.

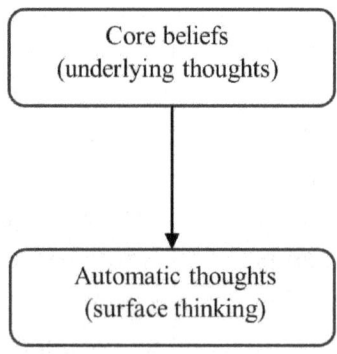

Figure 7: A diagram of the two levels of thought.

Automatic thoughts refer to the running commentary that goes through our heads as we go about our daily lives. If you pay attention, you will notice the constant chatter that goes on in your head about the things you are doing and how you are reacting to the people and events around you.

There is an easy exercise that will show you how this running commentary works. For the next minute, think about a bowl of fruit. Over the course of the minute, just let your thoughts do what they want as you think about a bowl of fruit. At the end of the minute, notice where your thoughts have taken you. Now consider the links between your starting point (thinking about a bowl of fruit) and where you ended up (thinking whatever it was you were thinking). Consider below how this might have played out for one individual. This person started thinking about a bowl of fruit and ended up thinking about arranging a meeting at work. Follow their automatic thoughts.

> *Ok. I'm thinking about a bowl of fruit. I can picture a bowl of fruit. It's got bananas in it. I like bananas. I should buy some next time I go to the supermarket. I also need to get a loaf of bread. I must start a shopping list. Pay attention and think about a bowl of fruit. Oh, and milk, I mustn't forget milk. I hate running out of milk. Someone said once that they have orange juice on their cereal instead of milk. Yuck. I couldn't imagine anything worse. Not that I eat much cereal. I should eat more cereal… it's probably good for you. I will put cereal on my shopping list. But that might be a waste because I probably won't eat it. I have bought lots of things I thought would be good for me, but I never ate them. That reminds me that I should clean out the pantry. I won't have time to clean out my pantry until after I finish my work project. Things have been so busy at work that I hardly get anything else done. That reminds me that I have to arrange a meeting with the project stakeholders when I get to work today.*

In contrast to our automatic thoughts, core beliefs refer to the underlying beliefs we have about how the world works and how we fit into that world. Core beliefs have influence on our automatic thoughts. That is, we think the things we do on the surface because of our underlying beliefs about how things work. Unlike automatic thoughts, the content of our core beliefs is not readily available to us but can be examined by considering the content of our automatic thoughts.

So, where do the logical errors in thinking we have been talking about fit into this conceptualisation? Let's consider that in the diagram below.

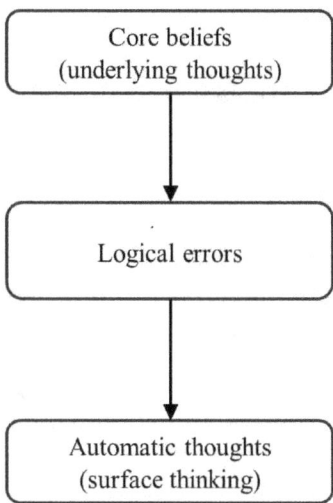

Figure 8: Where errors in thinking occur in our levels of thought.

The errors in thinking we make are a result of the core beliefs we hold. For example, if our core beliefs about the world and the future are that the world is threatening and the outlook is grim and pessimistic, then we are likely to inflate the degree of dangerousness we perceive and we are likely to catastrophise.

These logical errors then affect our surface thinking. We are more likely to be self-critical, or tell ourselves everything is hopeless, or tell ourselves that nothing is fair because of the logical errors we make based on our particular core beliefs.

Our core beliefs are built on the basis of a variety of influences. These include our genetic makeup (e.g., an inherited overly reactive nervous system), our experiences (the things that happen to us), the messages we receive (the things people have said to us or the way they have treated us), and the ways we have interpreted these events. If the influences are positive and healthy, our core beliefs tend to be clear, and logical errors are few. If the influences on us are negative, unhealthy or confusing, our core beliefs tend to be inaccurate, and the logical errors we make are many and strongly influence our automatic thoughts.

Underlying assumptions of logical errors

It has been suggested that each logical error is driven by a specific assumption. If our automatic thoughts are biased, then the biases are driven by our core beliefs and assumptions. Below are some examples of cognitive errors and examples of associated assumptions. Here we are referring to the assumptions that are inevitably made if the errors in our thinking are present.

Table 9: The assumptions underlying each logical error.

Cognitive error	Assumption
Filtering	The only events that matter are failures. I should measure myself by my errors.
Polarised thinking	Everything is always one extreme or the other.
Overgeneralisation	If it's true in one case, it must be true in every case that is even slightly similar.
Jumping to conclusions	If it has always been true in the past, it is going to be true in the future.
Catastrophising	Always think the worst because it is most likely to happen to you.
Personalisation	I am responsible for all bad things, failures, etc.
Control fallacies	You should be able to know in advance what is going to happen. You should have seen the bad thing coming before it happened.
Fallacy of fairness	The world is a fair place, and fairness influences how things turn out.
Blaming	Whether it is me or someone else, someone is always responsible when things are not the way I want them to be.
Shoulds	People have an obligation to do specific things that cannot be avoided.
Emotional reasoning	If a person feels bad, something must be wrong.
Fallacy of change	People must change to meet other people's needs.
Global labelling	A whole person and their entire life can be summed up by a single word (e.g., stupid).

Always being right	People have to choose a side, and there is a right side and a wrong side.
Heaven's reward fallacy	Choosing to do good things for others will oblige others to do good things in return.

Let's consider how these logical errors and the assumptions that are made affect automatic thoughts. Consider in this example what this person is saying to herself about the hostility she was experiencing from a neighbour.

> *I don't know what to do. I can't believe they are speaking to me like this. I don't even know what went wrong, but I must have done something... or not done something to cause this to happen* (personalisation). *I should have paid more attention or been kinder... or something* (shoulds). *I am always so hopeless, and I never get things right* (global labelling). *It serves me right. I deserve to be in this mess* (blaming). *I am now stuck in a situation where I worry every time I leave the house. I should have seen it coming and fixed it before things got this bad* (control fallacy).

Let's break this down and see where this person is making mistakes.

> Without even knowing why the neighbour was being hostile towards her, she has assumed that she is the one responsible – that there was something she could have done differently to achieve a better outcome (personalisation). It seems unreasonable for her to hold herself responsible when she did not even know why this occurred.

> Again, without knowing what has contributed to the problematic relationship with her neighbour, she comes up with a list of things she should have done, even though she did not know at the time that she was doing anything wrong (shoulds). It is all very well for her to say to herself that she should have done certain things, but we have to assume that if it was obvious that things needed to be done, she would have done them at the time.

> As a result of her version of her contribution to the relationship with the neighbour falling apart, she is self-critical and attributes certain characteristics to herself that attack her, not just in terms of the relationship problem, but in all things (global labelling). Even if she made mistakes in association with her neighbour, it does not mean that she is a bad or hopeless person deserving of bad things happening to her.

> Then, even though it was her neighbour who had commenced being hostile towards her and without knowing the reasons why this had happened, she holds herself responsible and thinks she deserves to have found herself in this difficult situation (blaming). She is pointing the finger at herself before having sufficient information to apportion responsibility.

> Finally, even though she does not understand what happened, she believes she should have acted in a way to prevent her relationship with her neighbour breaking down to the point of open hostility (control fallacy). This suggests that she should have magically known in advance what was going to happen and she should have or, indeed, could have controlled the end result.

The errors in this person's thinking have resulted in her feeling much worse than she would have felt if she had not made these errors. Let's find out how to change this way of thinking to protect yourself from the negative effects of logical errors.

Understanding automatic thoughts

The goal here is to teach you to think in a more realistic and balanced way so that you can cope better with difficult interactions with neighbours. This is done in a number of steps. Let's start this process.

Everybody experiences automatic thoughts. They reflect our way of making sense of and reacting to the world around us and to internal experiences, such as anxiety or memories and urges. Automatic thoughts are often highly believable, even when they are based on logical errors. As a result of their believability, we tend not to challenge them. If they pass unchallenged, they can have a profound and detrimental effect on our emotional state. For example, if a person thinks they are stupid and they do not challenge that thought, they are likely to feel upset and unworthy.

Consider this example.

> *How could I have been so stupid to trust my neighbour? I thought things were ok but then she up and ranted at me, accusing me of doing the wrong thing. I was stupid to believe everything was all right. I was stupid to think she was my friend. I was stupid to be tricked into thinking she was on my side. I was a fool. I am a fool.*

It would be hard to think this way without feeling bad as a consequence. We tend to believe the things we tell ourselves. Even when we do not pay much attention to our self-talk – our running commentary – we can still be affected by it.

Catching automatic thoughts

It is important to pay attention to your automatic thoughts so that their content can be used to identify both the logical errors you are making and, ultimately, your core beliefs. The way to go about this is to keep a thought record related to times when you notice a change in the way you are feeling.

In their simplest form, a thought record asks you to identify the event that has occurred, to take notice of the thoughts that go through your head at the time of the event, and to record the consequences you experience, both in terms of how you feel and how you might act in response. Consider the example below of a simple thought record.

A	B	C
Activating event	Belief or thought	Consequence: emotional and behavioural
Andrew said he was going to come over to my house to discuss resolving our difficulties but he didn't show up.	*I matter so little that he couldn't even be bothered turning up.*	*I felt so miserable I burst into tears.*
I heard that Andrew talked to a couple of our other neighbours to get them on his side in this dispute.	*No one likes me. Everyone will choose to be on Andrew's side and not mine.*	*I felt really down on myself. I sat alone and drank too much.*

We do not usually pay much attention to the thoughts that go through our heads, even though they can have such a profound effect on how we are feeling and what we choose to do as a result of feeling that way. To change our thinking, we have to learn to identify our automatic thoughts. When we consider the events that trigger a response in us, we can usually identify what went through our mind at the time.

By keeping track of your automatic thoughts, you can learn of patterns in your thinking that are linked with particular negative feelings and the behaviours you choose because you are feeling that way. Use the simple thought record below to keep track of your automatic thoughts in relation to events that stress you.

Simple automatic thoughts worksheet		
A	B	C
Activating event	Belief or thought	Consequence: emotional and behavioural

Worksheet available at elemen.com.au

Understanding and noticing logical errors

Everyone makes logical errors. It is important to understand this point. It is when the error you are making (e.g., everything should be fair) conflicts with how things really are (e.g., the world is neither fair nor unfair; it just is the way it is) that problems arise. It is important to be able to recognise the logical errors you are making so that you can correct them and correct the problems in your core beliefs. To do this, you can try the simple approach of expanding on your thought record form so that you include the types of logical errors that are reflected in your automatic thoughts.

Let's go back to our original thought record form and expand the examples.

Expanded thought record form - example			
A	B	C	D
Activating event	Belief or thought	Consequence: emotional and behavioural	Logical errors
Andrew said he was going to come over to my house to discuss resolving our difficulties but he didn't show up.	*I matter so little that he couldn't even be bothered turning up.*	*I felt so miserable I burst into tears.*	*Personalisation*
I heard that Andrew talked to a couple of our other neighbours to get them on his side in this dispute.	*No one likes me. Everyone will choose to be on Andrew's side and not mine.*	*I felt really down on myself. I sat alone and drank too much.*	*Jumping to conclusions*

In the first example, this person interpreted Andrew's failure to turn up or to let her know that he was not going to be able to make it as an indication that she was unworthy and of little value as a person. She personalised Andrew's rude behaviour. In the second example, she took a chat with neighbours on one occasion as evidence that she was losing all her friends. She jumped to the conclusion that just because Andrew spoke to neighbours, they would take his side and she would lose friends.

Below is an expanded thought record form that you can use to identify your logical errors in what you are thinking.

Expanded thought record form			
A	B	C	D
Activating event	Belief or thought	Consequence: emotional and behavioural	Logical errors

Worksheet available at elemen.com.au

Reframing your thoughts (cognitive restructuring)

Cognitive restructuring refers to challenging the content of our negative automatic thoughts. This is what we are trying to achieve here. The conclusions we reach because of our logical errors should be challenged and replaced with something that is healthier and more accurately reflects how the world really works.

Although there are lots of ways you can go about restructuring your thinking, we are going to introduce you to a straightforward method. We are going to start by ensuring that you understand the difference between fact and opinion. This is important as our thoughts and decision-making should be based on facts and not the opinions we form because of incorrect information that can underlie our core beliefs. For example, an opinion would be "I am stupid". You might form this opinion because someone has repeatedly told you that you are stupid or because they acted in a way that encouraged you to believe you were stupid. It is not the truth or a fact that you are stupid. It is a belief you have or an opinion you have formed because of incorrect information.

We refer to the opinion on which you rely as a work of fiction. That is, you write a story in your head about what is happening and then act as if the story is true. You need to be able to identify when you are relying on the story you have written in your mind rather than basing your thoughts on factual evidence. Let's start by having a go at identifying fact from opinion or fiction. In the spaces provided, you can add other things you have been thinking and consider whether they are facts or opinions.

Fact or fiction worksheet		
Statement	*Fact*	*Fiction*
I am stupid		√
I love bushwalking	√	
I am ugly		
I forgot to renew my driver's licence		
No one likes me		
This will be a disaster		
I'm not good enough		
All neighbours cause problems.		
I hate my job		
I should have known what was about to happen		
There are times when people feel stressed		

Checklist available at elemen.com.au

The facts here are:

> I love bushwalking
>
> I forgot to renew my driver's licence
>
> I hate my job
>
> There are times when people feel stressed

The statements that are opinions are:

> I am stupid
>
> I am ugly
>
> No one likes me
>
> This will be a disaster
>
> I'm not good enough
>
> All neighbours cause problems
>
> I should have known what was about to happen

Why should we make this distinction between what is a fact and what is an opinion? It is because the errors in thinking we make are based on opinion and not on fact. Further, because we hold this opinion, we assume that it is true because we are thinking it and not because it is based on fact.

To tidy up our thinking and remove the logical errors, we have to rely on those thoughts that are based on fact alone. We can reject thoughts that are just based on our opinions because our opinions can be faulty. Factual information will be a good guide for us to determine whether or not we should believe what we are thinking.

Cognitive restructuring worksheet - Example
What I am thinking *I think that no one like me and that everyone will choose Andrew's side, so I will have no friends.*
Facts supporting the thought *Andrew talked with a couple of our neighbours.*
Facts contradicting the thought *There is no indication that Andrew intended to turn our neighbours against me.* *These people have not indicated they do not wish to be friends with me.* *Other neighbours have offered to support me in this dispute.* *Friends outside of my neighbourhood have offered me lots of support.*
Is this thought based on factual evidence or opinion? *This thought that no one would like me and I would lose all my friends is just an opinion I formed because I was worried about Andrew talking to a couple of neighbours about our disagreement. This opinion doesn't take into account all my other neighbours and friends who support me and all of the friendly interactions I have had with neighbours after the chat between them and Andrew.*

By looking at the facts for and against a point of view being true, you can work out the value of holding that opinion. It seems like a waste of time to be thinking a particular thing and being negatively affected by it emotionally and behaviourally if you cannot even determine that the opinion reflects the truth. You can use the worksheet below to examine your thoughts in terms of the facts supporting what you are thinking and the facts that contradict what you are thinking.

Cognitive restructuring worksheet
What I am thinking
Facts supporting the thought
Facts contradicting the thought
Is this thought based on factual evidence or opinion?

Worksheet available at elemen.com.au

Rather than looking at facts for and against the truth of your thoughts, another very easy approach to reframing your thinking is what is called compassionate cognitive restructuring. Here, you are asked to look at your thoughts in a more compassionate way. Ask yourself what you would say to a person who was in a similar situation to you. In all likelihood, you would say something much kinder and closer to the truth than you are saying to yourself.

Consider this example.

Example	
Your friend says:	*Everyone will turn their backs on me, and I will have no friends in the neighbourhood.*
You might say:	*That's not true. You have good friendships in the neighbourhood, and people continue to support you. Your friendships are unlikely to be affected by a dispute with Andrew that has nothing to do with them.*

It is the case that we often are harder on ourselves than others think is necessary. We set higher standards. For example, you might say that you should never make a mistake and call yourself stupid if you do. Your friend would say that everyone makes mistakes and all we can do is learn from them.

It is interesting that, although you trust your good friends, you choose not to believe them when they make an honest, positive statement about you. Remember how it feels when the reverse occurs when you make a positive statement to your friend, and they dismiss what you say or reject it in favour of a statement you see as false. It is frustrating. You can be as kind and supportive to yourself as you are to the people you care about.

Making the restructured thinking habitual

To get to a point where you are thinking in a healthier way, you need to go through a process of deliberately challenging your thinking. You need to overlearn to notice your automatic thoughts and then reframe them into a healthier and more accurate alternative thought. You will then challenge your thinking and adjust your automatic thoughts without giving it much attention. Eventually, you will not even have to do that because your core beliefs will be corrected to offer you a more accurate template of how the world works and how you fit into that world.

Targeting the assumptions

Let's not forget about those assumptions that underlie the errors you make in your thinking. We need to challenge those assumptions to completely correct your thinking. Remember, if the assumptions that underlie the error are shown to be wrong, there is every reason to abandon the logical error and replace it with a more logical point of view.

There are a few ways you can challenge the assumptions that underlie logical errors. We are going to focus on three approaches. Firstly, we are going to apply the strategy of looking at the advantages and disadvantages of holding an assumption. Consider the following example of someone who is predicting that things are going to work out poorly.

Logical error and assumption
Catastrophising. Always think the worst because it is most likely to happen to you.

Advantages
I will always be on 'red alert' in case something happens.

Disadvantages
I will be on 'red alert' all the time, even when it is not necessary for me to be so.
I will find it hard to feel any joy about anything if I constantly worry about everything going wrong.
I will waste a lot of time worrying about things that end up not being as bad as I thought they were going to be.

Challenging the assumption that underlies a tendency to catastrophise, you can see that there are many more disadvantages to doing this than there are advantages. In fact, experiencing the disadvantages may turn out to be worse than the possible thing in the future you are worrying about.

Secondly, you can act against the assumptions. What would happen if the assumption was incorrect? Consider the following example.

Logical error and assumption
Catastrophising. Always think the worst because it is most likely to happen to you.

Thinks that might happen if I acted like the assumption was not true
I might be able to relax and feel calmer.
I might find some enjoyment in the things I do.
I might experience some peace of mind.
I might look forward to some things in the future.

By acting as if the assumption is false, you can usually identify the positive things that would occur as a consequence. All of these things are better than predicting a gloomy future. Remember, spending your time thinking about how badly things are likely to turn out in the future also removes all the pleasure from the present.

Finally, you can argue against the assumption. You can take the perspective that the assumption is wrong and develop an argument for your case. Consider the following example.

Logical error and assumption
Catastrophising. Always think the worst because it is most likely to happen to you.
Arguments against the assumption
Thinking something might happen will not make it happen.   *There is no cosmic force that is directing all bad things my way.*

Here, you are thinking of the *facts* that can be used to present a good argument that the assumption associated with the logical error is not accurate. This will allow you to challenge your error-ridden thinking and replace it with healthier thinking that will not encourage you to feel strong, negative emotions.

Below is a worksheet that will allow you to challenge the assumptions that underlie your errors in thinking.

Targeting assumptions worksheet
Logical error and assumption
Advantages
Disadvantages
Things that might happen if I acted like the assumption was not true
Arguments against the assumption

Worksheet is available at elemen.com.au

Here, we have asked you to consider challenging the sorts of thoughts you might have that are likely to make you feel worse than you would otherwise feel if you did not think that way. You have learned to access these logical errors by paying attention to your automatic thoughts that serve as the running commentary your mind provides. You have learned ways to challenge these errors and remove them and their influence from your thinking. The goal of doing these things has been to help you manage your distress and protect yourself from distress in the future.

Learning assertiveness skills

A useful focus of our attention is on assertive communication. We need to consider your assertiveness skills because you are likely to be faced with many challenging interactions that occur with a difficult neighbour. These may include putting your side of the case to them, asking them to cease engaging in a problematic behaviour, asking them to do something they are not currently doing, or working together to resolve a dispute.

Assertiveness refers to standing up for your rights without trampling over the rights of others. Some people mistake assertiveness for aggressiveness, which refers to aggressively pushing your rights irrespective of the rights of others. The other extreme is passivity, where a person will not stand up for their own rights and will allow others to walk over them.

So, the aim here is to teach you to stand up for your own rights without violating the rights of other people. An assertive interpersonal style will allow you to negotiate for what you want without demanding that it happen.

Asking for change

Firstly, we need to consider how to assertively solve problems by making reasonable requests for change or appropriate requests for what you would like to have happen. Many people find this difficult. They will start to make a request but are easily derailed by the deflection techniques used by the other person. Alternatively, they will start to make a request but are then affected by the annoyance you feel about the response of the other person. This following step-by-step guide is designed to help you plan ahead for how you are going to manage a request for change.

Define the problem situation

You should start by defining the problem you are facing. Do this by focusing on the facts of the matter and not your interpretation of the situation. You should do this by being as specific as possible. Avoid generalisations like "It's always the case…" or "Nothing ever goes right…". Instead, keep a narrow focus on the situation you have identified that you wish to change. Limit this to one problem at a time rather than bombarding the other person with a list of grievances.

> *Despite my repeated requests for you to make arrangements to cut back your tree that is destroying my fence, you have not done this.*

Describe how you are feeling

Here, you get a chance to describe how you feel about the situation. Remember, you are referring to how you feel and not how someone else *made* you feel. Be clear about the link between your feelings and the problem situation. Again, do not generalise to all situations or all problems.

Avoid blaming others. By blaming others, you put them on the defensive and little is ever resolved as a consequence. When you talk about how you are feeling, use what are called 'I messages'. That is, your descriptions of your feelings should start with something like "I feel…". No one can argue with you about this matter. They cannot say that you do not feel something that you have stated you feel. If you started with "You make me feel…", it is likely that the other person would argue that it was not their intention to make you feel that way, and if you do, that is your problem. Using 'I messages' allows you to avoid all of this discussion. In any case, you are the person who decides how you feel, and you should be able to relate that feeling to the other person.

This is a good opportunity to express your feelings. It is a mistake to assume that others know what you are thinking or feeling if you have not said so. If you have not said how you feel, the other person can do little more than guess. We make a mistake by assuming that someone who knows you well can 'mindread' and automatically know what you are thinking or feeling. Clear communication works much better than allowing others to guess.

> *I am disappointed that this arrangement hasn't been made and annoyed it has gone on for so long.*

Make your request for change

Here, you should make a statement about what you want to happen. You need to be brief. Do not turn your request into a lecture. Also, you need to be specific. Clearly state what you want rather than use terms that are not concrete. For example, it will not help to say, "I want things to improve" because that is a generalised statement that can be interpreted in a multitude of ways. You would be better off saying, "I want you to arrange to remove the tree" or "I want you to give me a realistic timeframe for cutting back the tree".

> *I want an arrangement made for you or someone you nominate to cut back the tree damaging my fence in the next seven days.*

Outline possible positive consequences

If the other person initially does not want to agree with your request for change, you may choose to point out the positive consequences that would follow from the agreement. Do not make wild promises. Just focus on the positive things that are likely to happen from the change you are requesting. You are building the argument for what you want. For example, you could say, "I want you to tell me the arrangement you have made to cut back the tree. If you do this, I will stop badgering you about the matter".

> *If you cut back the tree or arrange for someone to do it in the next seven days, I will take care of the repair of the fence myself at no cost to you.*

Outline potential negative consequences

If the other person is still reluctant to agree with what you are asking, you can outline the likely negative consequences for them if they choose not to comply with your wishes. Do not threaten. Simply state what you understand to be the bad things that will happen if things do not change.

It is important to remember that you should only outline negative consequences that you are certain you are willing to follow through on. You, too, have to live with the negative consequences so do not outline something you are not willing to do or have happen.

> *If you fail to cut back the tree or arrange for someone to cut back the tree in the next seven days, I will take the matter to the council and I will be seeking payment for the repair of the fence after the tree has been cut back.*

So, to summarise, when making a request for change, do the following:

- Define the problem situation
- Describe how you are feeling
- Make your request for change
- Outline possible positive consequences
- Outline potential negative consequences

This is a good approach to standing up for your rights in an assertive manner. It is relatively simple and straightforward. You can also work out in advance what it is you want to say and this protects you from having to make it up on the spot.

However, standing up for your rights may not be enough in itself if you are aiming for assertive communication. You need to be able to negotiate for what you want with a person who may be inclined not to give this to you. Consider the following negotiation process.

Learning negotiation skills

Often, the nature of the dispute with a neighbour will require that you reach some sort of agreement about how a situation might be resolved. This can feel like an overwhelming task, especially if you are not certain how a process of negotiation works.

Negotiating for what you want

To negotiate with another person, your starting point should be that you both have needs that are equally important. This will require some effort on your part. It is easy for us to assume that what we want is right and what the other person wants is wrong. However, if you hold this view, then any interaction about the issue in question will be an argument rather than a negotiation.

There are six steps that should be taken when you enter into a negotiation. Let's consider each of these steps.

Know what it is you want

Know what it is that you are negotiating for. You must have a clearly defined goal if you are to enter into a negotiation. If you are not clear about what you want, then how can the other person have any idea? It may take some thought on your part to clearly understand what it is you are trying to achieve. Take the time to clarify this in your own mind before moving forward.

Make a statement of what you want in specific terms

In specific terms and being as clear as possible, make a statement about what you want or do not want to happen. This can be in terms of what you want or do not want the other person to do. However, it may also be in terms of what you want as the outcome. For example, you may want an end to the escalation of tension between you and a neighbour.

Listen to the point of view of the other person

Your goal here is to understand the other person's perspective. To do this, you have to listen carefully to what the other person has to say about their point of view. You should use active listening skills where you can ask for clarification or elaboration rather than passively listen. Remember, you may not agree with the other person's perspective. What you should be doing is appreciating that they have a point of view that might be different from yours, but it is their point of view nonetheless.

Make a proposal

Next, you should make a proposal that offers a resolution. The proposal should not be solely based on what you want. It should take into account the other person's needs. This can be a challenging step that may take some thought on your part. It is easier to conceptualise a proposal that takes into account what both of you want if you approach it with the goal of achieving a 'win-win' outcome. This is where you get some of what you want, and the other person gets some of what they want. A win-win proposal has a much better chance of being accepted than a 'my way or the highway' approach.

Ask for a counterproposal

If your proposal is not accepted, do not be disheartened. Ask the other person for a counterproposal. Remember that your goal is to reach a point where you can both accept the proposal, even if you both do not get all of what you want.

Aim for compromise

The end result of any negotiation is typically a compromise. You are unlikely to get everything your way, but neither is the other person. You are aiming to reach a middle point that is satisfactory to you both. You give up some of what you want to gain some of what you want, and so does the other person.

Often, in a conflict, there are issues that have to be negotiated. You need to feel able to stand up for your rights and you need to be able to negotiate for an acceptable outcome.

Readiness to compromise

It is worth mentioning here that any negotiation is likely to be more successful if you enter into the negotiation in the right frame of mind. This requires that you approach a negotiation process feeling ready to compromise. We have some suggestions to increase your readiness to actively engage in a negation process.

Avoid blaming

Your readiness to compromise is increased if you do not use language that encourages blaming. This is because blame attribution tends to cause you to think of the other party as the enemy who has wronged you. Avoid statements such as, "You always…." Or "You never…". As we have mentioned before, replace this language with "I" statements such as, "I am concerned when … happens".

Also, to avoid blaming, it is worth considering carefully your own contribution to the escalating conflict. Acknowledge any mistakes you might have made. This encourages a mindset of compromise. It also encourages the other person to acknowledge their own actions.

Stay focused

Compromise is easier to achieve if you stay on topic. It is very easy to shift away from the reason you are having the discussion if the interactions become heated.

There is a thing called a 'content to process shift' that happens. This is where one person moves the discussion away from the content that is the focus of the discussion to other things that may or may not be related. For example, the reason for having the negotiation meeting may be discussed, but the conversation then moves to past difficulties or other issues that may or may not have been resolved and how that might have affected that person. So, what might start as a discussion of a fence dispute ends up being a discussion of how the person has felt about not being invited to a barbecue or not being consulted about an unrelated thing.

The end result of this process is that you spend time debating something that has little to do with what brought you to the negotiating table. In our example, the issue about the fence line dispute gets lost as the conversation moves away from the topic.

If you understand this process, you can identify when it happens. If someone else is doing it, you can bring them back to the topic that is the focus of discussion. For example, you might say, "That is an issue that might need to be discussed, but at the moment, we are talking about the problem of the fence." If you catch yourself doing it because it is an easy trap to fall into, check yourself and bring yourself back to the topic you are there to discuss.

Another point to be made is that it is important that you focus on the issue and not on the person. A negotiation process is not an opportunity to attack the other person. You will get further along with negotiations if you stay focused on the problem and not the person.

Be aware of differences

We have already discussed individual differences. It is worth remembering here that an awareness of these differences can make any negotiation easier and help you reach a compromise. Recognise that others might not see things the way you see them. Although you do not have to agree with their point of view, you can still appreciate the fact that people see things differently and understand the influences on that person that might have affected their perspective.

Mistakes can be made

An attitude that allows you to be open to compromise is one that understands that mistakes can be made and they are a normal part of life. There is no place at a negotiation table for shaming others or being shamed for mistakes that have been made. It is a simple truth that sometimes people make poor choices. There is no such thing as a perfect person.

Keep the peace and other orders

Although these are not the focus of this workbook, you have a variety of avenues available to you to access legal support to help manage a dispute you are having with a neighbour.

Legal avenues

Legal avenues are available to you if a neighbour has acted in a way that is a breach of law or a regulation. By seeking legal redress, you are taking the matter a step beyond an attempt to resolve the matter yourself or manage it in a way that suits you. In effect, by doing this, you are removing the matter from your direct control and handing that control to others. Of course, this may be an appropriate thing to do, especially in cases where the matter of the dispute is a serious one or in situations where you feel threatened.

In seeking legal support, you are looking for someone with more authority than you to force a neighbour to do something they are not yet doing, or not do something they are doing that is inappropriate.

Legal support can also be sought to protect you from harm. This may involve seeking a restraining order that would either require that the neighbour not approach you or that they be required to keep the peace. You should be aware that you would also have obligations in relation to these orders. These orders can have an influence on how you choose to act as, typically, there is an expectation that you do not approach the other party or that you also keep the peace.

When to pursue legal avenues

As stated, the appropriate time to seek a legal resolution is when a law or regulation has been breached, when all other resolution efforts have failed, and when you are feeling threatened by a neighbour's behaviour.

It is worth keeping in mind that seeking legal avenues for resolution can be costly, both in terms of the financial cost as well as the likelihood of permanent damage to your relationship with your neighbour. Even if the matter is found in your favour, it does not follow that your neighbour would be required to cover your legal costs.

Dispute resolution

There are often opportunities for you to engage in dispute resolution processes with a professional mediator. You may choose to engage in this process, or a court may recommend or order it.

If you seek outside assistance for the resolution of your dispute, you have to be open to the idea that it may play out differently than you expect. Dispute resolution processes typically involve a mediator whose job it is to act as a neutral third person. The mediator will guide the parties through the process of negotiating an outcome.

The mediator will set rules about how to conduct yourself during mediation sessions, and they will enforce those rules if they are breached. An example of a rule might relate to turn-taking in the discussions.

A mediator might meet with each party separately to assist them in understanding the problem from each person's perspective. However, they do not or should not take sides in the dispute.

It is the mediator's role to help both parties explore options for resolution. This may include generating ideas to resolve the dispute and discussion about the extent to which those options meet individual needs. The goal is to encourage compromise to reach an agreement where both parties are satisfied with the outcome.

Letting go of past hurts

There will come a point when it is time to move on from a disagreement with a neighbour. A time will come when you want to let go of the difficulties you have been experiencing and move on with your life. Here are some tips about how to let go of something that has consumed your thoughts for some time or has resulted in you having hurt feelings.

Change your self-talk

The things you say to yourself can influence how easy or difficult it is to move on from a problem with a neighbour. Consider the way you are viewing your experiences. If you are making errors in the way you are interpreting what has happened, clean up your thinking. Replace the errors in your thinking with more accurate thoughts about what has occurred or is likely to occur in the future.

Create psychological distance

See the problems with your neighbour as only one aspect of your life as a whole. Choose not to dwell on what has happened. If you catch yourself thinking about it, deliberately put that thought aside and replace it with something more relevant to some other aspect of your life or some other feature of your current existence.

Focus on yourself

By understanding that you have been through a difficult experience, you can allow yourself to focus on the things that you know make you feel better. By focusing on yourself, you draw your attention away from focusing on the person whose actions resulted in you feeling upset.

Be present focused

See the difficulties you have had with a neighbour in their historical context. That is, see those difficulties as something that happened to you but is not currently happening to you. When you catch yourself focusing on the past, deliberately turn your attention to something that is happening now that is not causing you any distress.

Be kind to yourself

Avoid criticising yourself for thoughts about past hurts that pop into your mind. Just acknowledge this happening as a normal reaction to having experienced a difficult time. Also, avoid going over what you might wish you had done differently. These things have already happened and cannot be changed. Comfort yourself that you are now wiser for the experience.

Express your emotions

If you need to express how you feel about what has happened, allow yourself to do so. Trying to suppress your emotional reactions can make them linger around for longer than they would if you expressed how you were feeling and then allowed yourself to let those feelings go.

Accept that others may not accept responsibility

Although it may feel difficult to achieve, learn to accept that the people who have hurt you may not apologise or change their behaviour in the future. You can still let go of past hurts even if they do not understand or accept their contribution to the problem. You can be in charge of your own reaction to something that has happened to you. It does not require someone else to change for you to do this.

Learn self-care

Think about what you need to feel all right and then do these things. By doing so, you are acknowledging that you have particular needs. You are the person who has the greatest understanding and knowledge about what is going to work for you in your attempts to feel better.

Seek out supportive people

Spend time with the people who support you the best. Choose the people who care about what happens to you and can offer you the things you need to feel supported and understood.

Learn to talk to others

An important part of letting go of past hurts is to talk about your experience. This helps you make sense of it. Listen to other people's perspectives on what has occurred. Then, allow yourself to move on. If your goal is not about accepting what has happened and moving on from it, you will find yourself going over and over the issues repeatedly. If your goal is to move on, you are likely to take time to reflect on what has happened and then let the matter go.

Consider forgiveness

As we have already identified, although you might expect an apology from the person you feel has wronged you, this apology may never come. Even if you do not receive an apology, you can still decide to forgive what someone has done in the past. This is something that you can choose to do without requiring any involvement from the other person. They will choose how they will handle the situation for themselves. You can be in charge of managing it the way you want.

Seek professional assistance if needed

If you are struggling to let go, you may wish to seek the advice of someone who is qualified to help you and has the professional experience and know-how to help you find ways to move forward.

Some final points

In finishing up, we would like to make some final points to remind you what you have learned.

> Although the other person in any dispute is responsible for the way they behave, you are the person who is responsible for what you do. Aim to make sensible choices that will de-escalate a conflict and/or protect you from harm.
>
> Understand that difficulties escalate when we feed off each other's behaviour or emotional reactions. This is characteristic of any conflict between people. However, you can choose to step away from this escalation and respond calmly and with clarity, even in cases where you are being provoked. By doing so, you are taking charge of your own situation.
>
> By understanding why people do what they do, you can adopt techniques that can have an influence on whether or not a person engages in a problematic behaviour.
>
> You can learn to control your emotional reactions and manage your anger and anxiety. This will allow you to minimise the effects of the difficult behaviour of a neighbour. These reactions tend to make us feel worse than we would do otherwise. Therefore, learning to control your reactions provides you with an opportunity to control how you feel.
>
> Do not fall into the traps caused by the errors in the way we think. By making errors in thinking, we create a situation where our problems are more challenging and harder to resolve.
>
> Learn to stand up for your rights in an assertive way. Avoid aggressive communication styles or passive responses to intimidation and bullying.
>
> Understand the value of negotiation and compromise. Learn negotiation skills and use them to resolve disputes.

We wish you well in resolving your problems.

Additional reading

Kennerley, H., Kirk, J., & Westbrook, D. (2016). *An introduction to cognitive behaviour therapy: Skills and applications (3rd edn.)*. London: Sage Publications.

Paterson, R.J. (2003). *The assertiveness workbook: How to express your ideas and stand up for yourself at work and in relationships.* London: New Harbinger Publications.

Tobin, D., Holroyd, K., Reynolds, R., & Wigal, J.K. (1989). The hierarchical structure of the Coping Strategies Inventory. *Cognitive Therapy and Research, 13(4),* 343-361.

www.ingramcontent.com/pod-product-compliance
Lightning Source LLC
Chambersburg PA
CBHW081521160426

43195CB00015B/2471